THE INTERNAL EFFECTS OF ASEAN EXTERNAL RELATIONS

Starting with a typology of ASEAN external agreements, the authors go on to provide an original reading of plurilateral agreements as 'joint' agreements. The book then offers both a clarification of the effects – direct or indirect – of external agreements within the legal orders of ASEAN Member States, and an explanation of the effects of external agreements within the legal regime of ASEAN. The authors conclude with a discussion of the role of ASEAN centrality and the role of the secretariat in shaping it.

INGO VENZKE is an Associate Professor in the Department of International and European Law at the University of Amsterdam.

LI-ANN THIO is a Professor in the Faculty of Law at the National University of Singapore.

T0384569

INTEGRATION THROUGH LAW
THE ROLE OF LAW AND THE RULE OF LAW
IN ASEAN INTEGRATION

General Editors
J. H. H. Weiler, European University Institute
Tan Hsien-Li, National University of Singapore

The Association of Southeast Asian Nations (ASEAN), comprising the ten member states of Brunei Darussalam, Cambodia, Indonesia, Lao PDR, Malaysia, Myanmar, Philippines, Singapore, Thailand and Vietnam, has undertaken intensified integration into the ASEAN Community through the Rule of Law and Institutions in its 2007 Charter. This innovative book series evaluates the community-building processes of ASEAN to date and offers a conceptual and policy toolkit for broader Asian thinking and planning of different legal and institutional models of economic and political regional integration in the region. Participating scholars have been divided up into six separate thematic strands. The books combine a mix of Asian and Western scholars.

Centre for International Law, National University of Singapore (CIL-NUS)

The Centre for International Law (CIL) was established in 2009 at the National University of Singapore's Bukit Timah Campus in response to the growing need for international law expertise and capacity building in the Asia-Pacific region. CIL is a university-wide research centre that focuses on multidisciplinary research and works with other NUS or external centres of research and academic excellence. In particular, CIL collaborates very closely with the NUS Faculty of Law.

THE INTERNAL EFFECTS OF ASEAN EXTERNAL RELATIONS

INGO VENZKE AND LI-ANN THIO

CAMBRIDGE
UNIVERSITY PRESS

University Printing House, Cambridge CB2 8BS, United Kingdom

Cambridge University Press is part of the University of Cambridge.

It furthers the University's mission by disseminating knowledge in the pursuit of education, learning and research at the highest international levels of excellence.

www.cambridge.org
Information on this title: www.cambridge.org/9781316606551

© Centre for International Law 2016

This publication is in copyright. Subject to statutory exception and to the provisions of relevant collective licensing agreements, no reproduction of any part may take place without the written permission of Cambridge University Press.

First published 2016

A catalogue record for this publication is available from the British Library

Library of Congress Cataloguing in Publication data
Names: Venzke, Ingo, author. | Thio, Li-ann, author.
Title: The internal effects of ASEAN external relations / Ingo Venzke, Li-ann Thio.
Description: Cambridge, United Kingdom : Cambridge University Press, 2016. | Series: Integration through law : the role of law and the rule of law in ASEAN integration | Includes bibliographical references and index.
Identifiers: LCCN 2016000901 | ISBN 9781316606551 (Paperback)
Subjects: LCSH: Law–Southeast Asia–International unification. | ASEAN. | Southeast Asia–Foreign relations. | Southeast Asia–Politics and government–1945-
Classification: LCC KNE168 .V46 2016 | DDC 341.24/73–dc23 LC record available at http://lccn.loc.gov/2016000901

ISBN 978-1-316-60655-1 Paperback

Cambridge University Press has no responsibility for the persistence or accuracy of URLs for external or third-party internet websites referred to in this publication, and does not guarantee that any content on such websites is, or will remain, accurate or appropriate.

CONTENTS

This monograph is published within the context of a wide-ranging research project entitled Integration Through Law: The Role of Law and the Rule of Law in ASEAN Integration (ITL), undertaken by the Centre for International Law at the National University of Singapore and directed by J. H. H. Weiler and Tan Hsien-Li.

The Preamble to the ASEAN Charter concludes with a single decision: "We, the Peoples of the Member States of the Association of Southeast Asian Nations ... [h]ereby decide to establish, through this Charter, the legal and institutional framework for ASEAN." For the first time in its history of over four decades, the Legal and the Institutional were brought to the forefront of ASEAN discourse.

The gravitas of the medium, a Charter: the substantive ambition of its content, the creation of three interlocking Communities, and the turn to law and institutions as instruments for realization provide ample justification for this wide-ranging project, to which this monograph is one contribution, examining ASEAN in a comparative context.

That same substantive and, indeed, political ambition means that any single study, illuminating as it may be, will cover but a fraction of the phenomena. Our modus operandi in this project was to create teams of researchers from Asia and elsewhere who would contribute individual monographs within an overall framework which we had designed. The project framework, involving several thematic clusters within each monograph, is thus determined by the framework and the place of each monograph within it.

As regards the specific content, however, the authors were free, indeed encouraged, to define their own understanding of the problem and their own methodology and reach their own conclusions. The thematic structure of the entire project may be found at the end of this Preface.

The project as a whole, and each monograph within it, display several methodological sensibilities.

First, law, in our view, can only be understood and evaluated when situated in its political and economic context. Thus, the first studies in the overall project design are intended to provide the political, economic, cultural and historical context against which one must understand ASEAN and are written by specialists in these respective disciplines. This context, to a greater or lesser degree, also informs the sensibility of each monograph. There are no "black letter law" studies to be found in this project and, indeed, even in the most technical of areas we encouraged our authors to make their writing accessible to readers of diverse disciplines.

Comparative experience suggests that the success of achieving some of the more ambitious objectives outlined in Article 1 of the Charter will depend in no small measure on the effectiveness of legal principles, legal rules and legal institutions. This is particularly true as regards the success of establishing "an ASEAN Community comprising the ASEAN Security Community, the ASEAN Economic Community and the ASEAN Socio-Cultural Community as provided for in the Bali Declaration of ASEAN Concord II". Article 2(2)(n) stipulates the commitment of ASEAN Member States to act in accordance with the principle of "adherence to multilateral trade rules and ASEAN's rules-based regimes for effective implementation of economic commitments and progressive reduction towards elimination of all barriers to regional economic integration." The ASEAN Member States therefore envisage that rules of law and the Rule of Law will become a major feature in the future of ASEAN.

Although, as seen, the Charter understands itself as providing an institutional and legal framework for ASEAN, the question of the "role of law and the rule of law" is not advocacy but a genuine enquiry in the various substantive areas of the project as to:

- the substantive legal principles and substantive rules of the various ASEAN communities;
- the procedural legal principles and rules governing institutional structures and decision-making processes;
- implementation, enforcement and dispute settlement.

One should not expect a mechanical application of this scheme in each study; rather, a sensibility that refuses to content itself with legal enactments as such and looks to a "living" notion of law and institutions is ubiquitous in all the studies. Likewise, the project is sensitive to "non Law." It variously attempts to locate the appropriate province of the law in this experience. That is, not only the role of law, but also the areas that are and should remain outside the reach of legal institutionalization with due sensitivity to ASEAN and Asian particularism and political and cultural identities.

The project, and the monographs of which it is made, are not normatively thick. They do not advocate. They are designed, for the most part, to offer reflection, discuss the pros and cons, and in this way enrich public awareness, deepen understanding of different options and in that respect contribute indirectly to policymaking.

This decisive development of ASEAN has been accompanied by a growing Asian interest in various legal and institutional forms of transnational economic and political cooperation, notably the various voices discussing and showing an interest in an East Asia Integration project. The number of Free Trade Agreements (FTAs) and Regional Trade Agreements (RTAs) has increased from six in 1991 to 166 in 2013, with a further 62 in various stages of negotiations.

Methodologically, the project and many of the monographs are comparative in their orientation. Comparative law is one of the few real-life laboratories that we have in which to assess and understand the operation of different legal and institutional models designed to tackle similar objectives and problems. One should not need to put one's own hand in the fire to learn that it scorches. With that in mind a couple of monographs offer both conceptual reflection and pragmatic "tool boxing" on some of the key elements featuring in all regional integration systems.

Comparative law is in part about divergence: it is a potent tool and means to understand one's own uniqueness. One understands better the uniqueness of Apples by comparing them to Oranges. You understand better the specialness of a Toyota by comparing it to a Ford.

Comparative law is also about convergence: it is a potent tool and means to understand how what are seemingly different phenomena are part of a broader trend, an insight which may enhance both self-understanding and policy potentialities.

Although many studies in the project could have almost immediate policy implications, as would the project as a whole, this is not its only or even principal purpose. There is a rich theory of federalism which covers many countries around the world. There is an equally rich theory of European integration, which has been associated with the advent Union. There is also considerable learning on Free Trade Areas and the like.

To date, the study of the legal aspects of ASEAN specifically and other forms of Asian legal integration has been derivative of, and dependent on, theoretical and conceptual insight which were developed in different contexts.

One principal objective of ITL and these monographs will be to put in place the building blocks for an authentic body of ASEAN and Asian integration theory developed in, and with sensitivity to, the particularities and peculiarities of the region and continent. A theory and conceptual framework of Asian legal integration will signal the coming of age of research of and in the region itself.

Although the monographs form part of an over-arching project, we asked our authors to write each as a "standalone" – not assuming that their readers would have consulted any of the other titles. Indeed, the project is rich and few will read all monographs. We encourage readers to pick and choose from the various monographs and design their own menu. There is, on occasion, some overlap in providing, for example, background information on ASEAN in different studies. That is not only inevitable but desirable in a project of this amplitude.

The world is increasingly witnessing a phenomenon of interlocking regional organization where the experience of one feeds on the others. In some way, the intellectual, disciplinary and comparative sensibility of this project is a microcosm of the world it describes.

The range of topics covered in this series comprises:

The General Architecture and Aspirations of ASEAN

The Governance and Management of ASEAN: Instruments, Institutions, Monitoring, Compliance and Dispute Resolution

Legal Regimes in ASEAN

The ASEAN Economic Community

ASEAN and the World

The Substantive Law of ASEAN

ACKNOWLEDGEMENTS

We are indebted to the co-directors of the project 'ASEAN Integration Through Law', Professors Joseph H.H. Weiler and Michael Ewing-Chow, as well as executive director Dr. Hsien-Li Tan. They offered valuable guidance, support, comments and suggestions while writing this contribution.

We thank the participants of the workshop in Amsterdam on ASEAN external relations (July 2012) and Martine van Trigt for her assistance. We are furthermore grateful to our commentators at the Singapore workshop (August 2012), Professors Marise Cremona and Jürgen Rüland, for their helpful critiques. Professor André Nollkaemper has read the manuscript at a later stage, and Christiane Ahlborn commented on parts – many thanks to both.

We thank Chen Zhida for his assistance with research and Tatevik Manucharyan for her help in meticulously formatting the text and finalizing it.

AAF	ASEAN Automotive Federation
AANZFTA	ASEAN-Australia-New Zealand Free Trade Area
ACT	ASEAN Council of Teachers
AICHR	ASEAN Inter-Governmental Commission for Human Rights
AKFTA	ASEAN-Korea Free Trade Area
ARIO	Articles on the Responsibility of International Organizations
ASEAN	Association of Southeast Asian Nations
ASG	ASEAN Secretary-General
BITs	Bilateral Investment Treaties
CEDAW	Convention to Eliminate All Forms of Discrimination Against Women
CMCF	Communications and Multimedia Content Forum
DSM	Dispute Settlement Mechanism
ECHR	European Convention on Human Rights
ECtHR	European Court of Human Rights
EEC	European Economic Community
EPG	Eminent Persons' Group
GATT	General Agreement on Tariffs and Trade
GFP	Gender Focal Points
GMAGs	Gender Mainstreaming Action Groups

IACHR	Inter-American Convention on Human Rights
ICCPR	International Covenant on Civil and Political Rights
ICSID	International Center for the Settlement of Investment Disputes
ILC	International Law Commission
IO	International Organisation
IPA	Inter-Parliamentary Assembly
ITA	International Tin Agreement
ITC	International Tin Council
JCC	Joint Cooperation Committee
MCW	Magna Carta of Women
MNCWA	Myanmar National Committee for Women's Affairs
MOU	Memorandum of Understanding
MoWA	Ministry of Women's Affairs
MOWE	Ministry of Women Empowerment
MWFCD	Ministry of Women, Family and Community Development
NCAW	National Committee for the Advancement of Women
NCRFW	National Commission on the Role of Filipino Women
ONCWA	National Commission on Women's Affairs
PCIJ	Permanent Court of International Justice
PoA	plan of action
PRC	People's Republic of China
ROK	Republic of Korea
SEOM	Senior Economic Officials Meeting
TAC	Treaty of Amity and Cooperation

TOR	Terms of Reference
UDHR	Universal Declaration of Human Rights
UNAT	UN Administrative Tribunal
VCCR	Vienna Convention on Consular Relations
VCLT	Vienna Convention on the Law of Treaties

Chapter 1

Introduction and parameters of inquiry

This contribution sets out the legal effects of ASEAN external agreements within ASEAN Member States, with regard to the relationship between ASEAN as an International Organisation and its members. In particular, it demonstrates how ASEAN practice in relation to its external relations is, on the whole, likely to contribute to an increased role for the ASEAN Secretariat.

In approaching the theme of internal effects of external agreements, we distinguish three types of agreements. First, agreements which ASEAN concludes as an International Organisation. Such agreements do not bind Member States and do not show internal effects within domestic legal orders. However, they might strengthen the monitoring and facilitating functions of the Secretariat in relation to Member States' treaty obligations and thus have internal effects within the ASEAN legal order or, better expressed, as we will argue, its legal *regime.*

Agreements with non-ASEAN Member States usually take the form of international treaties between state parties, which is the second type of agreement. Such agreements may well be read in a rather uncontroversial manner to suggest plainly that they are plurilateral agreements indistinguishable from other international law agreements. There is nothing specific about them when it comes to internal effects or otherwise. We discuss their internal effects within Member

1

States from the points of view of both international law and, in a comparative perspective, domestic constitutional law. Since knowledge about the constitutional practices of ASEAN Member States with regard to the internal effects of international law is uneven and in any event rather sparse, this part of the argument largely models different possibilities. As yet, we do not have sufficiently evolved case-studies on the internal effects of these plurilateral agreements. We draw on ASEAN Member States' domestic practices to the extent that we could gather it. We note, and are aware, that our access and thus knowledge is distributed unevenly, with most references stemming from the Singapore context. In light of the need for further studies in this regard, for now, we further engage in a specific case study of the implementation of the Convention to Eliminate All Forms of Discrimination Against Women (CEDAW). We do so for inspiration and by proxy, believing that this is illuminating and helpful for readers in imagining what impact ASEAN plurilateral legal relations might have. Finally, to note in regard to plurilateral agreements, we do pay tribute to the classical distinction between monism and dualism. But we argue that the actual practice of states frequently converges on matters such as how international law influences the interpretation of domestic law, even if it is not directly applicable.

The third and final type of agreements that we distinguish is, in fact, a second way of reading those international treaties between ASEAN states and third states. It notably credits the fact that a sub-group of contracting parties together form ASEAN. We call the treaties 'joint ASEAN agreements' and draw attention to a series of features that justify treating them as something distinct and specific. Such features include the fact that the treaties are signed by ASEAN members in one column and by the other party (or parties) in another. In addition, some agreements have modalities of entering into force or modalities of termination suggesting that ASEAN Member States need to act jointly. The first reading of the agreements would look at those features as immaterial symbolism. We suggest that they do matter more than that and will support that suggestion in our reading of these agreements as 'joint ASEAN agreements'.

Where it concerns the direct effect of joint ASEAN agreements within the legal orders of the Member States, it is true that on the whole, these do not differ from plurilateral agreements and general international law. However, owing to obligations of membership and the principle of ASEAN centrality – two factors which we will explain in further detail below[1] – their indirect effects are likely to be stronger. Furthermore, they impact the relationship between ASEAN as a separate entity and its members. In particular, they trigger the Secretariat's functions of monitoring and facilitating compliance.

The contribution proceeds by setting out the further parameters and backgrounds to our enquiry (Chapter 2). This involves a first reading of the ASEAN Charter and a discussion of the prospects of further legalisation. We see this section as a necessary lead-up to asking whether it might be justified to speak of an 'ASEAN legal order' and what that might mean. It is in light of that discussion that we introduce

[1] See Section 6.2.

the slightly less ambitious and more fitting notion of an ASEAN legal regime. We further introduce the three types of external agreements in a succinct overview (Chapter 3) and then discuss each in turn. Chapter 4 focuses on agreements that ASEAN concludes as an International Organisation. It provides an introduction to ASEAN's external relation powers and argues that Member States are not bound by these agreements, absent a more specific provision to that effect in the Charter.

Chapter 5 then approaches the heart of the matter: the effect of external agreements within Member States. It offers an introduction which seeks to clarify key terms in the debate and first sets out the view from international law in this regard (5.1). It argues that general doctrine and jurisprudence do not demand that international law be given any specific domestic effect. Specific legal regimes, however, might require particular implementing action, specifically, enabling and conforming domestic legislation. However, contrary to the view from European Law, international law does not generally require that its provisions be given direct effect (5.2). A comparison with the view from European Law clarifies that part of the argument (5.3).

Domestic law might of course grant certain international law norms direct effect in the absence of an international legal obligation to do so. We approach the view from domestic law first in terms of monism and dualism (5.4), but then suggest that domestic legal systems often converge with respect to their treatment of international law, especially in the indirect effect they give to it; that is, in the way it matters for the construction of domestic statues (5.5). Since there is considerable flux in how domestic legal practice actually deals with international law – something that the broad concepts of monism and dualism hardly capture – we close this section with a discussion of the policy considerations that could further inform how domestic law treats international law. As noted, we model possibilities at this stage, which we support with references to the domestic practices of ASEAN Member States. We do not as yet have the necessary access to the constitutional doctrine of all ASEAN Member States which would be needed to support a more concrete and comparative analysis (5.6). For now, we turn to a case study in Chapter 6 on the internal effects of the CEDAW which offers a concrete application of the broader argument. Through examining this field of law, we are able to glean ASEAN Member States' attitudes towards international law and its internal effects; it offers clues on how they will approach the internal effects of ASEAN external agreements.

Chapter 7 introduces and distinguishes joint ASEAN agreements from other international treaties. It first further clarifies what we mean by joint ASEAN agreements, by distinguishing them from the European Union practice of 'mixed agreements' (7.1). We then offer evidence that supports singling them out as specific or distinct agreements (7.2), and we draw attention to the consequences that they have in terms of internal effects (7.3). We distinguish two levels of those effects. The first pertains to the relationship between the institution of ASEAN as an International Organisation and its Member States. Those are the effects within the ASEAN legal regime. In particular, we see a number of functions that accrue to the Secretariat by virtue of ASEAN's external relations practice (7.4). We also turn to the ASEAN Summit in that regard and draw out the implications of joint ASEAN agreements for dispute settlement processes (7.5). In conclusion, we summarise and commit to reading at least some of ASEAN's external agreements as joint agreements (Chapter 8).

Chapter 2

Contextualising ASEAN

Our enquiry is set against the broader theme of how political and legal cultures provide incentives and constraints on creating a legal regime within the ASEAN sub-regional context. Specific factors in this regard include the rich variety between its members in terms of political systems. Within the ten ASEAN states, the polities range from the authoritarian to the more democratic. They notably include socialist regimes (Vietnam, Laos), Westminster-influenced parliamentary democracies (Malaysia, Singapore), a Malay Muslim monarchy (Brunei), polities dominated by the military (Myanmar), and secular presidential-based systems (Indonesia, Philippines) where the influence of religion on public life is a significant factor. Given the diversity in terms of politics, ethnicity, culture, languages, colonial history and levels of development, it is not surprising that pragmatism and functionalism were the key unifying forces extant within ASEAN.

Key to the later turn to a more rules-based regime was the desire of ASEAN and its Member States for deeper regional integration, which was complicated by the persistence to a large degree of the 'ASEAN Way' or a non-legalistic, diplomatic approach towards managing international relations. In this section we thus sketch the trajectory ASEAN has embarked upon towards the goals of legal integration, and the institutions it has set up, before approaching the question of whether it is at all justified to speak of an ASEAN legal order or legal regime and what that might mean.

2.1 ASEAN Charter: continuity or rupture?

With the advent of the ASEAN Charter, which was adopted at the 13th ASEAN Summit in 2007 and entered into force in December 2008, the question arises as to whether a new form of governance has taken shape. Does it confirm, modify or supersede what has been described as the 'ASEAN Way'? To some extent, the ASEAN Charter was designed to signal a shift from the 'ASEAN Way' in international affairs. All the same, it may be more accurate to view its contents as a confirmation of existing practice, or an evolutionary modification pursuant to deeper regional integration, particularly economic integration.[1] The 'ASEAN Way' has been the time-honoured *modus operandi* governing the conduct of ASEAN members since the creation of the grouping on 8 August 1967. How do relational governance and a rule-oriented approach towards institutionalised co-operation inter-relate? To what extent have relationships undergone institutionalisation, measured against the common markers of binding legal obligation, precision (such that the parties know what conduct is required or prohibited), and

---

[1] L. Chun Hung, 'ASEAN Charter: Deeper Regional Integration under International Law' (2010) 9 *Chinese Journal of International Law* 821–837; L. Leviter, 'The ASEAN Charter: ASEAN's Failure or Member Failure?' (2010) 43 *Journal of International Law and Politics* 159–210.

delegation to an autonomous agent for monitoring and enforcement?[2]

The twin pillars of the 'ASEAN Way' rested on *musyawarah* (discussion and consultation) and *mufakat* (consensus-seeking). This commitment to reach decisions by consensus and consultation would avoid the need to take a formal vote or follow a procedure. As Paul Davidson described it:

> Relations based governance relies on the personal relationship of the actors to establish the parameters of their cooperation; agreements are based on the mutual relations of the actors and depend on knowledge of and familiarity with each other ... maintenance of good relations is relied on for the 'enforcement' of commitments.[3]

Further, there was a desire to handle things in a fraternal (within the family) manner through the dominant method of quiet diplomacy and a resistance towards ceding sovereignty to an international or supranational body. This is reflected in

---

[2] For those three factors see J. Goldstein, M. Kahler, R. D. Keohane and A.-M. Slaughter, 'Introduction: Legalization and World Politics' (2000) 54 *International Organization* 385–399. For the argument that they fall short in capturing the broader and more subtle sociological dynamics of socialization see M. Finnemore and S. Toope, 'Alternatives to "Legalization": Richer Views of Law and Politics' (2001) 55 *International Organization* 743–758; now also F. Kratochwil, *The Status of Law in World Society: Meditations on the Role and Rule of Law* (Cambridge: Cambridge University Press, 2014) 32–33.

[3] P. J. Davidson, 'The Role of International Law in the Governance of International Economic Relations in ASEAN' (2008) 12 *Singapore Year Book of International Law* 213–224, at 214.

the six principles contained in the 1976 Treaty of Amity and Cooperation (TAC)[4]. A 1987 Protocol opened the TAC to accession by other states in Southeast Asia and beyond.[5] These principles are contained in Article 2 TAC:

a. Mutual respect for the independence, sovereignty, equality, territorial integrity and national identity of all nations;
b. The right of every State to lead its national existence free from external interference, subversion or coercion;
c. Non-interference in the internal affairs of one another;
d. Settlement of differences or disputes by peaceful means;
e. Renunciation of the threat or use of force;
f. Effective cooperation among themselves.

Despite the adherence to the cardinal ASEAN principle of non-interference in internal affairs[6] as a manifestation of the international law principle of sovereign equality, which formerly justified turning a blind eye to, e.g. human rights abuses in a member state, this was never strictly adhered to and has gradually been relaxed.[7] One might add that ASEAN Member

---

[4] Treaty of Amity and Cooperation in Southeast Asia, Bali, Indonesia, 24 February 1976.

[5] To date these include China, India, Japan, Pakistan, South Korea, Russia, New Zealand, Mongolia, Australia, France, East Timor, Bangladesh, Sri Lanka, North Korea, the European Union and the United States.

[6] Art. 2(2)(e) ASEAN Charter.

[7] See e.g. ASEAN criticism against Myanmar's government crackdown on protesting monks in August 2007, Statement by ASEAN Chair (September 2007) at www.aseansec.org/20974.htm (references to 'flexible' and 'constructive' engagement). Consider also Art. 2(2)(g) ASEAN Charter, which calls for 'enhanced consultation on matters seriously affecting the common interest of ASEAN'.

States have differed on which of these behavioural principles they emphasize: socialist and military regimes have typically underscored non-interference in national affairs, while other Member States have foregrounded institutional cooperation and friendly relations.

Some argue that the 'ASEAN Way' will continue but be supplemented or modified by a new rule of law (adherence to rules) culture where greater reliance is placed on rules, institutions and procedures to regulate conduct, with the motivation to achieve efficient and predictable action.[8] The ASEAN legal order or regime certainly cannot be likened to a whole-hearted embrace of European supranationalism, but it may be argued that it is more than an arena for the conduct of diplomacy or managed politics. In the course of this contribution, we will show increasingly strong indicators that point towards a rising role for the ASEAN Secretariat in external relations. It already is much more than an arena.

Competing factors will certainly continue to tug and pull on the characterisation of ASEAN and its further development.[9] Like so many institutions, it occupies a middle way

[8] T. Koh, W. Woon and C. Sze-Wei, 'Charter Makes ASEAN Stronger, More United and Effective' *Straits Times (Singapore)*, 8 August 2007. The Kuala Lumpur Declaration on the Establishment of the ASEAN Charter (12 December 2005) provides that 'the ASEAN Charter will codify all ASEAN norms, rules and values and reaffirm that ASEAN agreements signed and other instruments adopted before the establishment of the ASEAN Charter shall continue to apply and be legally binding where appropriate.'

[9] For an overview of the competing forces and widely diverging assessments as well as forecasts, see A. Jetschke, 'ASEAN', in M. Beeson and R. Stubbs (eds.), *Routledge Handbook of Asian Regionalism* (Abingdon, Oxon: Routledge, 2012) 327–337.

between legal and political orderings of regional affairs; a mixture of formal and informal structures and operations. It has recourse to both legal obligations and 'soft law' or aspirational standards. In fact, it is often criticised for looking much better on paper than in practice when it comes to increased institutionalisation.[10]

It will be in this way of mixes between formal and informal mechanisms that we approach the internal effects of ASEAN external relations. We are not only concerned with the effect of hard external commitments, but also with governance mechanisms such as reporting, channelling information and monitoring. In what follows, we continue by providing further background to our theme and discuss main features of the institutional set-up as envisaged by the ASEAN Charter. A further examination of the Charter yields both elements of continuity and (modest) departure from ASEAN as it presented itself before.

2.2 The consensus rule

'Consultation and consensus' remains the basic principle of decision-making according to Article 20(1) ASEAN Charter. If decisions are taken by consensus, as opposed to a voting procedure, this questions the idea that ASEAN as a legal entity has a will that is separate from its members. It rather affirms that it lacks genuine independence and that it is

---

[10] *Ibid.* at 331 ('There is some movement towards greater autonomy of the organization, but the reforms look better on paper than in practice').

unable to act autonomously of its Member States.[11] The existence of a separate will is commonly taken to be necessary for any international organisation with legal personality.[12]

For the first forty years of its existence, ASEAN was not an international 'actor' but an 'arena'[13] or forum where ASEAN Member States interacted and collaborated, with ASEAN being described as an 'institution without legalization',[14] underscoring the observation that 'Asians just do not do law, at least of the international kind.'[15] As such, the perception was that 'ASEAN has not generally been associated with international law and treaties.'[16] The operating of

---

[11] While other international or supranational organizations also operate on the basis of consensus which does not require unanimity, within the ASEAN context, there was pre-2007 no procedure for breaking through an impasse caused by a lack of consensus. On the conditions for independence from the perspective of political science see Y. Z. Haftel and A. Thompson, 'The Independence of International Organizations: Concept and Applications' (2006) 50 *Journal of Conflict Resolution* 253–275.

[12] N. D. White, *The Law of International Organizations*, 2nd edn. (Manchester: Manchester University Press, 2005) 1–2, 68; also with reference to H. Schermers and N. M. Blokker, *International Institutional Law*, 4th edn. (Leiden: Martinus Nijhoff, 2003) 34.

[13] On competing conceptualizations of international organizations along those lines see C. Archer, *International Organizations*, 3rd edn. (London: Routledge, 2001) 68–87; C. Schruer, 'The Waning of the Sovereign State: Towards a New Paradigm for International Law?' (1993) 4 *European Journal of International Law* 447–471; J. Klabbers, 'Two Concepts of International Organization' (2005) 2 *International Organization Law Review* 277–293.

[14] M. Kahler, 'Legalization as Strategy: The Asia-Pacific Case' (2000) 54 *International Organization* 549–571.

[15] *Ibid.* at 551–559.   [16] Davidson, 'The Role of International Law', 216.

ASEAN in the key of politics rather than law was reflected in its insistence upon the principle of sovereign equality,[17] as regional 'economic growth, social progress and cultural development' was to be facilitated through 'joint endeavours in the spirit of equality and partnership'.[18]

The degree to which consensus is dominant, however, depends on the specific type of activity involved. For example, the dominance of a consensus-oriented model would be apparent in the field of human rights. The weak institutions established under Article 14 ASEAN Charter, which simply provided that 'ASEAN shall establish an ASEAN human rights body' with the ASEAN Foreign Ministers setting its terms of reference (TOR), reflect an unwillingness to grant autonomy to ASEAN institutions.

The ASEAN Inter-Governmental Commission for Human Rights (AICHR) is composed of government representatives[19] and is a consultative body with essentially promotional functions and no coercive powers. While tasked with promoting and protecting human rights (and upholding the Universal Declaration of Human Rights, the 1993 Vienna

---

[17] Art. 5, ASEAN Charter ('Member States shall have equal rights and obligations under this Charter.') and Art. 30(2), in relation to equal contributions to the operational budget of the ASEAN Secretariat. This pegs contributions at the level of the financial capabilities of its weakest member, Laos. (EPG original proposal was to peg it to economic strength but this was rejected)

[18] The ASEAN Declaration (Bangkok Declaration) Bangkok, 8 August 1967.

[19] AICHR TOR, 5. Each Representative in the discharge of his duties 'shall act impartially' and enjoys necessary immunities and privileges.

Declaration and ratified human rights treaties[20]), it is charged to do so in a non-confrontational manner, with due respect for 'national and regional particularities',[21] state sovereignty and non-interference in internal affairs[22] and to 'enhance regional cooperation'.[23] A 'constructive and non-confrontational' approach is mandated, as an evolutionary approach to standard-setting.[24] Its primary mandate is to develop strategies, engage in some human rights standard-setting, undertake educational, dialogical and advisory activities and to report to the ASEAN Foreign Ministers Meeting.[25] Following Article 20 ASEAN Charter, AICHR decision-making shall be based on consultation and consensus. Its budget has to be approved by the ASEAN Foreign Ministers Meeting[26] and AICHR is afforded secretarial support from the ASEAN Secretariat,[27] as opposed to having its own dedicated staff. A political solution is preferred in relation to any difference arising out of the interpretation of the AICHR TOR, as this is referred to the ASEAN Foreign Ministers Meeting for a decision.[28]

Conversely, the ASEAN Charter has modified the consensus rule to some extent. Article 20(3) provides that the consensus-oriented rule does not apply where an ASEAN legal instrument stipulates its own decision-making method. It also provide for a channel for taking a decision to break an

---

[20] AICHR TOR, 1.6.   [21] AICHR TOR, 1.4.
[22] AICHR TOR, 2.1. (Principles)   [23] AICHR TOR, 1.5.
[24] AICHR TOR, 2.4, 2.5.   [25] AICHR TOR, 4.   [26] AICHR TOR, 8.
[27] AICHR TOR, 7.2. This is funded by the ASEAN Secretariat's annual operational budget: 8.8.
[28] AICHR TOR, 9.8.

impasse, by providing that the ASEAN Summit 'may decide how a specific decision can be made', which notably does not preclude the possibility of voting.[29]

There is at least a shy willingness to depart from the consensus rule in other fields relating to security or economic issues. In relation to economic commitments,[30] the 'ASEAN Minus X' formula allows for 'flexible participation'.[31] This is a concession to effective action. The formula shall also ensure that 'the pace of integration should not always be determined by the lowest common denominator or the slowest member (...). Members who are ready to move first in particular areas should be free to do so, provided the door is left open for others to join when they are ready.'[32] That is the case, for example in the ASEAN-Korea Free Trade Area (AKFTA),[33] which was established according to the Framework Agreement on Comprehensive

[29] Note that some agree that 'the degree of autonomy enjoyed by international organisations ultimately depends on the possibility of adopting decisions by majority.' T. Gazzini, 'The relationship between international legal personality and the autonomy of international organisations', in E. Collins and N. White (eds.), *International Organizations and the Idea of Autonomy: Institutional Independence in the International Legal Order* (Abingdon, Oxon: Routledge, 2011) 97–141.

[30] The EPG had not confined its recommendation for a more flexible approach towards decision-making merely to economic matters.

[31] Art. 21(2) ASEAN Charter.

[32] Minister for Foreign Affairs (George Yeo), 83 Singapore Parliament Reports, 17 September 2007 (ASEAN Integration).

[33] Agreement on Trade in Goods under the Framework Agreement on Comprehensive Economic Cooperation among the Governments of the Member Countries of the Association of Southeast Asian Nations and the Republic of Korea.

Economic Cooperation.[34] In this context, six ASEAN countries (Brunei, Indonesia, Malaysia, Philippines, Singapore, Thailand) as well as Korea agreed to eliminate tariffs for 90% of all products by 2010. In departing from a strict rule that any move ahead needs to be based on the consensus of all parties, this new practice of allowing ASEAN members to participate at different speeds recognises the differing capacities of individual Member States.

2.3 Towards legalisation

In the scholarly literature, ASEAN has been the subject of what has been described as the 'under-legalisation thesis'.[35] With the nuances that we have already described, its members have shown an aversion to law and formal institutions. Hortatory standards in informal instruments are favoured over binding legal rules mandating specific forms of behaviour or obligation. Disputes are managed with the help of quiet diplomacy and consultation, rather than adversarial litigation. This reflects the prioritisation of harmonious, 'quasi-familial' relations which places a premium on consensus and compromise, through what is known as the 'ASEAN

---

[34] This expressly provides for 'special and differential treatment and additional flexibility' for the new ASEAN countries of Cambodia, Laos, Myanmar and Vietnam (CLMV), recognizing the 'different stages of economic development'. Art 5.3 provides for Implementing Committee (AEM + Korea) www.aseansec.org/18063.htm.

[35] J. E. Alvarez, 'Institutionalised Legislation and the Asia-Pacific Region' (2007) 5 *New Zealand Journal of Public and International Law* 9–28.

Way', with its relational emphasis on informality, personal ties (关系 *guanxi*) and soft-law-based governance.

The adoption of the ASEAN Charter in 2007 was hailed as a turn towards a more rules-based regime, a move from regional cooperation towards integration, an attempt to dovetail the 'appearance and reality' of ASEAN as an international organisation pursuant to intensifying regional integration.[36] The avowed goal was to facilitate cooperation over matters relating to security, trade, economic integration and also a more people-centric ASEAN committed to development and human welfare. This would be pursuant to the vision of ASEAN 2020, articulated in 1997 of ASEAN as 'a concert of Southeast Asian nations, outward looking, living in peace, stability and prosperity, bonded together in partnership in dynamic development and in a community of caring societies'.[37]

The Eminent Persons' Group (EPG), which was tasked to make recommendations with respect to drafting the ASEAN Charter to serve the ASEAN legal and institutional framework, identified ASEAN's primary problem as lacking institutions and procedures to monitor, implement and enforce ASEAN norms. It urged that ASEAN 'must have a culture of commitment to honour and implement decisions, agreements and timelines'.[38] To that end, it recommended

---

[36] D. Seah, 'The ASEAN Charter' (Current Developments) (2009) 58 *International and Comparative Law Quarterly* 212–219.

[37] ASEAN Vision, 2020, available at: www.aseansec.org/1814.htm.

[38] Para 6, Report of the Eminent Persons Group on the ASEAN Charter (Dec 2006), available at www.aseansec.org/19247.pdf.

that to take its obligations seriously, a Dispute Settlement Mechanism (DSM) 'be established in all fields of ASEAN cooperation which should include compliance monitoring, advisory, consultation as well as enforcement mechanisms'. Further, the ASEAN Secretariat should notably be entrusted with 'monitoring compliance with ASEAN agreements and action plans, with the Secretary-General of ASEAN reporting its findings to the ASEAN Council and the Community Councils on regular basis'.[39] In a 'radical departure'[40] from past practice, the EPG recommended that the ASEAN Council 'should have the power to take measures to redress cases of serious breaches of ASEAN's objectives, major principles and commitments to important agreements', such as suspending rights and privileges of membership, and possibly, expulsion.

While these recommendations were not wholly endorsed, the ASEAN Charter did reflect many of them. For one thing, the Charter expressly confers legal personality[41] upon ASEAN and provides that rights and duties contained

---

[39] Para 6, Report of the Eminent Persons Group on the ASEAN Charter.

[40] A. Duxbury, 'Moving Towards or Turning Away from Institutions?' (2007) 11 *Singapore Year Book of International Law* 177–193, at 189.

[41] Art. 3 ASEAN Charter (raising questions about its IO responsibility and the residual responsibility of ASEAN Member States to third parties; the continued dominance of 'consensus' is indicative of 'separate entity' problems: i.e. how to have distinct responsibility etc. if all depends on consensus of component members?). This does not mean that ASEAN did not have legal personality prior to 2007 or necessarily that it now has it in a meaningful way. This would depend on its functions and powers. See in further detail S. Chesterman, 'Does ASEAN Exist? The Association of Southeast Asian Nations as an International Legal Person' (2008) 12 *Singapore Year Book of International Law* 199–211.

in the Charter shall prevail over other ASEAN instruments in the event of inconsistency.[42] Member States are required under Article 5 to 'take all necessary measures including the enactment of appropriate domestic legislation' to implement Charter provisions and to comply with membership obligations.[43] With the entry into force of the Charter, all ASEAN Member States have undertaken to uphold its purposes, which include developing ASEAN as a rules-based organisation.

Remarkably, however, these developments towards legalisation are not paralleled by revisions of the mandate of the ASEAN Secretariat, which was established in 1976 and whose mandate was only last updated in 1992. And still:

> The ASEAN Secretariat's vision is that by 2015, it will be the nerve centre of a strong and confident ASEAN Community that is globally respected for acting in full compliance with its Charter and in the best interest of its people.[44]

It thus espouses a strong vision and a new mission but runs on a low budget, with very limited resources. Its capabilities have not kept apace with its expanded role – expansionism without expense. We will highlight numerous examples of how external relations endow the ASEAN Secretariat with a

---

[42] Art. 52(2) ASEAN Charter.

[43] The Charter is silent as to whether it can take effect directly. There is no uniform approach amongst ASEAN states in relation to whether treaties are self-executing or non self-executing: D. A. Desierto, 'ASEAN's Constitutionalization of International Law: Challenges to Evolution Under the New ASEAN Charter' (2010) 49 *Columbia Journal of Transnational Law* 268–320 at 300–303.

[44] www.asean.org/asean/asean-secretariat (last accessed 26 March 2014).

series of governance functions. This is not an entirely new phenomenon, but with increasing external relations activity it is a sharply increasing one. For the Secretariat to actually fulfill only a fraction of the tasks that it is endowed with or those that lie within its reach, its capacities need to grow accordingly.

With respect to the issue of Dispute Settlement, stressed by the EPG, this is now dealt with in Chapter VIII of the ASEAN Charter. It sets out frameworks for amicable settlement, including the good offices, conciliation or mediation that the ASEAN Secretary-General or the Chairman of ASEAN may offer. Disputes concerning the application or interpretation of ASEAN agreements continue to be resolved on the basis of the Treaty of Amity and Cooperation of 1976. For economic agreements, however, an enhanced dispute settlement mechanism is available according to the 2004 Protocol.[45] A 2010 Protocol[46] to the Charter spells out a stricter dispute settlement mechanism that may be applicable across the board, unless provided otherwise. It sets out that consultations need to be held within a fixed time-frame and further paves the way for dispute settlement by an arbitral tribunal. As of now, however, the 2010 Protocol has not yet entered into force.[47]

---

[45] ASEAN Protocol on Enhanced Dispute Settlement Mechanism, Vientiane, Lao PDR, 29 November 2004.

[46] 2010 Protocol to the ASEAN Charter on Dispute Settlement Mechanisms, Ha Noi, Vietnam, 8 April 2010.

[47] It requires the ratification of all ASEAN Member States to do so. See for the current state of affairs http://cil.nus.edu.sg/2010/2010-protocol-to-the-asean-charter-on-dispute-settlement-mechanisms/ (last accessed 26 March 2014).

The trajectory for the future development of a 'politically cohesive, economically integrated and socially responsible'[48] ASEAN Community has been laid out in the Roadmap for an ASEAN Community (2009–2015)[49] which contains three 'blueprints': the ASEAN Political-Security Community, Economic Community and Socio-Cultural Community Blueprint.

Finally, while the Charter adopted a trajectory of continuity by reiterating existing ASEAN principles,[50] it incorporated a commitment to 'thicker' value-laden principles such as human rights, democracy and the rule of law, as well as regional economic integration, in a market-driven economy, in the form of a formal treaty.[51] This is a considerable expansion of ASEAN's original primary concern with trade and security, evident in its founding document, the 1967 Bangkok Declaration, a political instrument.[52]

---

[48] Preamble ASEAN Charter

[49] ASEAN Secretariat, April 2009, available at www.asean.org/resources/publications/asean-publications/item/roadmap-for-an-asean-community-2009-2015.

[50] Art 2(1) ASEAN Charter ('reaffirm and adhere to the fundamental principles' in existing ASEAN treaties and other instruments).

[51] Art. 2(2)(h)(i), and (n) ASEAN Charter.

[52] The five founding members are Indonesia, Philippines, Singapore, Thailand and Malaysia. Subsequently, it reached its current size of ten when Brunei (7 January 1984), Vietnam (28 July 1995), Laos and Mynamar (23 July 1997) and Cambodia (30 April 1999) joined ASEAN. (Comment: East Timor). See R. C. Severino, *Southeast Asia in Search of an ASEAN Community: Insights from the Former ASEAN Secretary-General* (Singapore: ISEAS Publishing, 2006) at 57–67. Full text available at http://cil.nus.edu.sg/rp/pdf/1967%20ASEAN%20Declaration-pdf.pdf.

2.4 Institutional set-up by comparison

When discussing the internal effects of ASEAN's external relations, we will on occasion refer to the law of the European Union (EU). We wish to contrast ASEAN and the EU at this stage so as to highlight the significant differences. Such a comparison also helps to further clarify ASEAN's own institutional set-up. To be sure, we do not believe that ASEAN approximates European regional integration. The EU can enter into external agreements that bind Member States, its law can be enforced by supranational organs acting on their own initiative and domestic institutions directly apply Union law and recognize its primacy over domestic law.[53] These core elements of the European legal order rest on a whole range of cultural, political and legal pre-requisites that are lacking, weak or only slowly taking shape within the ASEAN context. Differences are manifold. Among other things, the scheme of EU law rests on a significant conferral of competences from members to the supranational organisation that is simply absent in the ASEAN context.[54] Further key points of distinction include the following:

– The European Commission is an actor in its own right and within the realm of Union competence, it can conclude external agreements that, subject to the ordinary legislative

---

[53] For an overview see P. Craig and G. de Búrca, *EU Law*, 4th edn. (Oxford: Oxford University Press, 2007) 268–378.

[54] See further *Ibid* at 95–100; A. von Bogdandy and J. Bast, 'The Federal Order of Competences', in A. von Bogdandy and J. Bast (eds.), *Principles of EU Constitutional Law* (Oxford and Munich: Hart and Beck, 2009) 275–308.

procedure, are then binding on the Union and its Member States. Member States are bound to such external agreements by virtue of the commitments they have made under the European treaties.[55] The Commission concludes most external agreements together with Member States as 'mixed agreements' where each act within their own spheres of competence.[56]

- The EU has comprehensive legislative and treaty-making powers drawn from its Member States and constitutes its own legal order. It sets itself apart from international law.[57]
- Union law demands, under certain conditions to be given direct effect within the domestic legal order of Member States of the EU. In particular domestic courts thereby practically implement and enforce Union law (complementing the Union institutions themselves).[58]
- One driving force behind these developments has been the European Court of Justice (ECJ), which enjoys comparatively broad competences that include infringement procedures against Member States typically brought by the

---

[55] Art. 216(2) TFEU: 'Agreements concluded by the Union are binding upon the institutions of the Union and on its Member States.'
[56] See in further detail, Chapter 6.
[57] The formative seminal cases are Case 26/62, *Van Gend & Loos* [1963] ECR 1, and Case 181/73, *Haegeman v Belgium* [1974] ECR 449. See in further detail A. von Bogdandy and M. Smrkolj, 'European Community and Union Law and International Law', in R. Wolfrum (ed.), *Max Planck Encyclopedia of Public International Law* (Oxford: Oxford University Press, 2012).
[58] J. H. H. Weiler, 'The Transformation of Europe' (1991) 100 *Yale Law Journal* 2403–2483.

Commission (and exceptionally by other Member States)[59] and actions for annulment of secondary legislation (which can also be brought by individuals and then go to the General Court in the first instance).[60] The ECJ also receives references for preliminary rulings from Member State courts on matters concerning EU law,[61] which has had far-reaching consequences for the EU legal order.[62]

What kind of internal effects of external agreements are we then talking about, given the differences between European and South East Asian integration?

2.5 An 'ASEAN legal order' or an 'ASEAN legal regime'?

For agreements that the EU itself concludes, the focus would rest on the effect of international law within the EU legal order as a separate legal layer between international law and the law of the Member States.[63] A discussion of the internal

---

[59] Art. 258 Treaty on the Functioning of the European Union (TFEU).

[60] Art. 263 TFEU.   [61] Art. 267 TFEU.

[62] Weiler, 'The Transformation of Europe'.

[63] See P. J. Kuijper '"It Shall Contribute to . . . the Strict Observance and Development of International Law. . ." The Role of the Court of Justice', in A. Rosas, E. Levits and Y. Bot (eds.), *The Court of Justice and the Construction of Europe* (The Hague: T.M.C. Asser Press 2013) 589–612; C. Eckes, 'International law as law of the EU: The role of the European Court of Justice' in E. Cannizzaro, P. Palchetti and R. A. Wessel (eds.), *International Law as Law of the European Union* (The Hague: Martinus Nijhoff, 2012) 353–377; B. de Witte, 'Direct Effect, Primacy and the Nature

effect of economic agreements such as the General Agreement on Tariffs and Trade (GATT) would thus centre on their effect within EU law as an autonomous legal order.[64] Member State institutions do not even have a say in this question, nor is there direct contact between Member States' legal orders and the GATT. That contact is mediated by the layer of EU law and its institutions.

We contend that there is no similar ASEAN legal order as a separate and autonomous layer of legal obligations to speak of. Asking about the internal effects of ASEAN external relations thus pertains primarily to the effects of international agreements within ASEAN Member States. There might, on this account, not be anything distinctive about ASEAN external agreements when compared to general international law. But that is not the whole story. There also exist the legal relationships between ASEAN as a distinct entity and its Member States; those, too, may be termed internal, even if they do not set themselves apart from international law as a distinct legal order. Because it has not thickened into a separate legal order and is unlikely to do so any time soon, we wish to speak of the *ASEAN legal regime*. Speaking of a regime also allows us to continue

of the Legal Order', in G. de Búrca and P. Craig (eds.), *The Evolution of European Union Law* (Oxford: Oxford University Press, 2011) 323.

[64] A. Tancredi, 'On the absence of direct effect of the WTO dispute settlement body's decisions in the EU legal order', in E. Cannizzaro, P. Palchetti and R. A. Wessel (eds.), *International Law as Law of the European Union* (The Hague: Martinus Nijhoff, 2012) 249–268; M. Mendes, *The Legal Effects of EU Agreements* (Oxford: Oxford University Press, 2013) 174–249.

examining the effects and channels of influence that are not strictly legal.[65]

We will further argue that joint ASEAN external agreements affect the role of the ASEAN Secretariat and its relationship with the Member States. They thus show internal effects within the ASEAN legal regime. Even if there is no separate layer of ASEAN law that mediates the effects of international law, we cautiously suggest that compliance with ASEAN external agreements could qualify as an obligation of membership within ASEAN. They could thus have an internal effect in this sense of becoming 'internalised' through membership obligations.

The internal effects of external relations – be it within Member States or in the relationship between ASEAN as an international organisation and its Member States – in any event, hinges on a number of parameters. At its most foundational level, it hinges on the type of external agreement or, where interpretative leeway exists, what we make of those agreements.

---

[65] We think of regime in Steven Krasner's seminal formulation as a set of explicit or implicit 'principles, norms, rules, and decision making procedures around which actor expectations converge in a given issue-area'. S. D. Krasner, 'Structural Causes and Regime Consequences: Regimes as Intervening Variables' (1982) 36 *International Organization* 185–205, 185.

Chapter 3

Types of external agreements

When speaking of the internal effects of ASEAN external agreements, it is important to identify and distinguish the range of such agreements. It is certainly not uncommon for legal instruments associated with ASEAN or for commentators to speak of ASEAN agreements in an undifferentiated manner, lumping together under this heading not only clearly different kinds of external agreements, but also agreements between ASEAN Member States alone. As a first qualification, it is evident from the subject and ambition of our inquiry that we are only concerned with *external* agreements – instruments whose parties include at least one party in addition to some ASEAN states or ASEAN as an international organisation. But even then, we encounter within the umbrella category of 'external agreements' instruments that differ widely with regard to their legal nature and what concerns the parties involved. There are, in particular, two different bases that would qualify for a typology of external agreements, in order to add further clarity.

The first would entail revisiting the spectrum of hard and soft obligations, in terms of the bindingness of these norms, their specificity and any mechanisms of enforcement or compliance. With regard to their legal nature, ASEAN external practices create instruments ranging on a scale from laudatory and hortatory declarations with no apparent ambition to create legal obligations, on the one hand, and agreements to create clear treaty commitments, on the other hand. When it comes to hard commitments, most of ASEAN external relations do indeed take the form of agreements between ASEAN Member States and one or more third parties. Other instruments, which involve ASEAN as an international organisation and which leave out any direct involvement of the Member States tend to impose weaker obligations.

On that basis, speaking about the internal effects of ASEAN external relations, we would need to distinguish between instruments such as the *Agreement between the Governments of the Member Countries of the Association of Southeast Asian Nations and the Government of the Russian Federation on Economic and Development Cooperation*, which is an international treaty signed and ratified by its eleven state parties, from instruments like the *Memorandum of Understanding between the Association of Southeast Asian Nations (ASEAN) and the United Nations (UN) on ASEAN–UN Cooperation*, signed by the respective Secretary-Generals of these organisations at that time, Ong Keng Yong and Ban Ki Moon. The first is a classic treaty that gives rise to hard law, while the latter is best described as a soft law instrument.

At the same time, we recognise that internal legal effects may well arise from practices of external relations that do not take the outward form of international treaties and that do not, on the face of it, purport to create legal obligations. The functions that a range of MOUs ascribe to the ASEAN Secretariat are a case in point. This is why we conceive of their legal nature as resting on a spectrum.[1] Legal

normativity does not come in two watertight binary compart-
ments of 'binding' and 'non-binding'.[2] We consider it prudent
to include formally non-binding instruments and practices of
ASEAN's external relations in our study not only because they
are ubiquitous in the activities of ASEAN, but also because
research in other contexts has repeatedly shown that they do
have internal legal effects. We take this spectrum of hard and
soft agreements into consideration, but ultimately build our
threefold typology of external agreements on another basis.

Such an alternative, second basis distinguishes external agreements according to the parties involved. To this end,
we differentiate between *agreements of ASEAN as an international organisation* with any other party, *plurilateral treaties* involving only state parties, and a third type that involves
both ASEAN as an IO and its Member States, together with
third parties. It is questionable, but often times also not really
decisive, whether ASEAN as a distinct entity is party to the
agreement. We call this third type of external agreements
joint ASEAN agreements.[3]

---

[1] See K. W. Abbott and D. Snidal, Hard and Soft Law in International
Governance (2000) 54 *International Organization* 421–456; J. Pauwelyn,
R. Wessel, and J. Wouters (eds.), *Informal International Lawmaking*
(Oxford: Oxford University Press, 2012).

[2] M. Goldmann, 'We Need to Cut Off the Head of the King: Past, Present,
and Future Approaches to International Soft Law' (2012) 25 *Leiden
Journal of International Law* 335–368.

[3] This is in line with the contribution by M. Cremona, P. Venesson and
R. Lee 'The External Agreements of ASEAN – Inventory and Typology',
ASEAN ITL Project, Draft (2013).

Sometimes these types are clear-cut and there is little room to argue about which kind of agreement we are facing. In many cases, however, different readings are possible and a lot then depends on what to make of an agreement. ASEAN's external practice is in considerable flux and likely to be shaped by the persuasiveness of one reading rather than another. We will show that the grey area between a few clear-cut cases is considerable and that for this large area of different shades of grey, a conceptualisation of ASEAN external practices as 'joint ASEAN' has more purchase and potential than first meets the eye.

The remainder of this section briefly introduces the three types of agreements. The following sections then discuss them in further detail and with emphasis on their internal effects.

3.1 Agreements by ASEAN as an IO

The first type of external agreements includes those entered into by ASEAN as an IO and not by ASEAN Member States.[4] On the other side of such agreements are typically other IOs. One example is the *Cooperation Agreement between the Association of Southeast Asian Nations (ASEAN Secretariat) and the International Labor Office,*[5] signed by the Secretary-General

---

[4] See also MOU between ASEAN Secretariat and ESCAP Secretariat (2002); MOU: ASEAN Secretariat and SCO Secretariat (2005); MOU for Administrative Arrangements: ASEAN Secretariat and ADB (2006).

[5] 20 March 2007, www.ilo.org/public/english/bureau/leg/download/asean .pdf (last accessed 15 July 2013).

of ASEAN and the Director-General of ILO. This Cooperation Agreement pursues the aim of facilitating collaboration between both agencies through dialogue and information exchange in a manner consistent with the policies, rules and regulations of the respective organisations (Article 5(1)). The agreement does not seem to have any domestic implications for any of the Member States of either organisation. When asked about the significance of this Cooperation Agreement, the Singapore Manpower Minister stated before the Parliament:

> The Cooperation Agreement, which was signed between ASEAN and ILO recently, reflects the strong commitment of both organizations to collaborate closely in addressing labour and employment issues as well as promoting social progress. Singapore is supportive of this Cooperation Agreement and believes that it will pave the way for increased cooperation and partnership between ASEAN and ILO through mutual exchange of information and joint technical cooperation projects. Such collaboration is likely to benefit workers across ASEAN.[6]

While such agreements are indeed unlikely to show internal effect within Member States in any immediate way, they may, however, have an effect on the relationship between ASEAN and members in more subtle ways by boosting the governance functions of the Secretariat. The project between ASEAN, the ILO and Japan concerning industrial relations may serve as a case in point. The project was funded by Japan and

---

[6] Gan Kim Yong (Minister for Manpower), *Sing.,* Parliamentary Debates, vol. 83, col. 24 (09 Apr 2007) Cooperation Agreement between ASEAN and ILO (Significance and Impact).

implemented within ASEAN Member States jointly by the ASEAN and ILO Secretariats under the Cooperation Agreement of March 2007.

Where there are disputes between IOs over the implementation of a MOU such as the *MOU between the ASEAN Secretariat and the UN Office on Drugs and Crimes, on Drug Control and Crime Prevention Cooperation*, these are mostly to be 'settled amicably through consultation and negotiation between the ASEAN Secretariat and the Office on Drugs and Crime'.[7] Agreements by ASEAN as an IO do not create obligations or institutional mechanisms that go beyond that.

3.2 Plurilateral agreements

Plurilateral agreements are treaties between ten states who are members of ASEAN and at least one third state party. All eleven or more parties are equal and are treated in the same manner. Exceptionally, there may also be a smaller number of participating ASEAN Member States. This type of agreements were certainly typical of the pre-Charter external relations practice. A post-Charter example is the 2010 *Agreement on Cultural Cooperation between the Governments of Southeast Asian Nations and the Government of the Russian Federation* or the *Agreement on Dispute Settlement Mechanism under the*

---

[7] Art IX, MOU between the ASEAN Secretariat and the UN Office on Drugs and Crimes, on Drug Control and Crime Prevention Cooperation; Article VI, Agreement of Co-operation between the ASEAN and the UNESCO 1998.

Framework Agreement on Comprehensive Economic Cooperation between the ASEAN and the Republic of India.

Several features and practices support a reading of these and other external agreements as plainly plurilateral agreements between a number of state parties. For instance, in 2010 Indonesia tried to protect local industries by delaying a tariff reduction on some 228 items and by seeking to renegotiate the terms of the *ASEAN-China Free Trade Agreement.*[8] Indonesia here acted like any state party would do in any plurilateral agreement. The fact that it was an ASEAN Member State did not seem to bear on its practice. Non-ASEAN parties behave likewise. Were Indonesia to breach any treaty commitment, non-ASEAN state parties could take legal countermeasure against Indonesia, but not against other ASEAN Member States.

3.3 Joint ASEAN agreements

It is interesting to note that many agreements involving ten or slightly fewer ASEAN Member States and other state parties, in one way or another, pay tribute to the fact that ASEAN Member States are involved. The treaties just mentioned as examples of plurilateral agreements already recognise this in the title, which does not list all state parties, but instead names the non-ASEAN state party, on one side, and ASEAN, on the other. The way they are signed follows that division as well. The signatures of all eleven state parties are not

[8] ASEAN-China Free Trade Area: Not a Zero-Sum Game, ASEAN Secretariat, 7 January 2010.

arranged alphabetically, but the ten ASEAN Members sign alphabetically in a left column and the third party in a separate column.

On a first reading, this may be immaterial and regarded as inconsequential symbolism. We do not think that this is the case. Sometimes there are rather explicit manifestations of difference. For example, the *Framework Agreement on Trade in Goods with India* (2009), signed in the way just described, provides in Article 24 that termination must be by written notice, whether from India or from 'ASEAN Member States collectively'.[9] It seems as though a single ASEAN Member State could not proceed to request termination by written notice. It is further interesting to note that other agreements specify that the ASEAN Secretary-General shall act as depository for all ASEAN Member States.[10]

Other agreements, which we group in this third type of external agreements, could involve ASEAN as an IO in addition to ASEAN Member States and a third party.

---

[9] See also Art. 80(2) 2008 Agreement on Comprehensive Economic Partnership among Japan and Member States of the Association of Southeast Asian Nations: '2. This Agreement shall terminate either when all ASEAN Member States which are Parties withdraw in accordance with paragraph 1 or when Japan does so.'

[10] See, e.g, Art. 78 Agreement on Comprehensive Economic Partnership among Japan and Member States of the Association of Southeast Asian Nations (2008), 'For the ASEAN Member States, this Agreement including its amendments shall be deposited with the Secretary-General of ASEAN, who shall promptly furnish a certified copy thereof, to each ASEAN Member State.'

Chapter 4

Agreements of ASEAN as an international organisation

This section deals with the first kind of agreements that are concluded by ASEAN as an International Organisation and not by its Member States. It offers an introduction to the external relations powers of ASEAN, especially its Secretariat. It then argues that such agreements cannot bind Member States absent a provision to that effect in the Charter. As we will discuss in this chapter's final part, members can well bear concurrent and subsidiary responsibility and they can incur indirect liability for international wrongful acts of ASEAN. The external relations of ASEAN as an IO thus impact its internal relations with its members.[1]

4.1 Introductory note on the Secretariat

The functions and role of the Secretariat and the ASEAN Secretary-General (ASG) are primarily managerial. The ASG is the Chief Administrative Officer of ASEAN[2] and is

---

[1] Cf. M. Hirsch, *The Responsibility of International Organizations Toward Third Parties: Some Basic Principles* (Dordrecht: Martinus Nijhoff, 1995) at 178 (concluding that 'the rules of responsibility on the external level occasionally have significant implications on the internal plane of an organization').

[2] Art. 2(3) ASEAN Charter.

appointed by the ASEAN Summit for a single non-renewable term of five years. According to Article 29 ASEAN Charter it falls onto the Secretariat to ensure and maintain 'budgetary discipline', 'sound financial management policies', and financial procedures consistent with international standards. Article 30 moreover charges the ASG with preparing the Secretariat's annual operating budget for the approval of the ASEAN Coordinating Council, upon recommendation of the committee of permanent representatives.

The ASG is to serve 'as spokesman and representative of ASEAN on all matters' in the absence of a contrary decision of the Chairman of the Standing Committee. The ASG is further to conduct consultations with contracting parties, the private sector, NGOs and other ASEAN constituencies, as well as coordinate dialogues with international and regional organisations and any dialogue country.[3] The ASG also acts as the 'channel of formal communications'[4] between ASEAN Committees, bodies and the Secretariat and other IOs and governments.

The distinct role of the ASEAN Secretary in relation to the Member States is reflected in several provisions relating to the obligations, which members owe to ASEAN as an IO. Some degree of institutional autonomy is sought by Article 30, which states that the ASEAN Member States should through 'equal annual contributions' remitted in a

---

[3] Art. 5 (a)–(c) Protocol Amending the Agreement on the Establishment of the ASEAN Secretariat, Manila, 22 July 1992.

[4] Section 7, Protocol Amending the Agreement on the Establishment of the ASEAN Secretariat, Manila, 22 July 1992.

'timely manner' provide the ASEAN Secretariat with 'the
necessary financial resources to perform its functions effectively'. However, funding is pegged at the lowest level by
requiring equal funding, as opposed to funding based on
the different wealth levels of each Member. Here we see again
the strong emphasis placed on the principle of equality
between Member States. The wealth levels, as measured by
GDP or income per capita, are truly significant and weaker
members might fear that the power of the purse leads to too
imbalanced and undue influence.[5] Furthermore, members
are obliged under Article 11 'to respect the exclusively
ASEAN Character' of the Secretary-General's responsibilities
and 'not to seek to influence them in the discharge of their
responsibilities'.

4.2 Other ASEAN actors in external relations

Article 41 ASEAN Charter sets out that Member States, in the
conduct of the external relations of ASEAN, seek to 'develop
common positions and pursue joint actions' based on 'unity
and solidarity' and so present a unified position in external
relations. ASEAN Foreign Ministers Meetings are designed 'to
ensure consistency and coherence in the conduct of ASEAN's
external relations'.

Member States take turns as Country Coordinators
to hold 'overall responsibility in coordinating and promoting

---

[5] See International Monetary Fund, Asia and Pacific: Leading the Global
Recovery, Balancing for the Medium Term, World Economic and
Financial Surveys, April 2010.

the interests of ASEAN in its relations with the relevant dialogue partners, regional and international organizations and institutions . . .'[6] Article 42(2)(a) of the ASEAN Charter provides that these Country Coordinators *represent* ASEAN in relations with the external partners and co-chair meetings with external partners. There are several declarations and MOUs signed by the host Member State, acting as Country Coordinator, on behalf of ASEAN including:

- MOU between ASEAN and the Government of Australia on the ASEAN-Australian Economic Cooperation Program (AAECP) Phase III 1994, signed by H.E. Dr. Surin Pitsuwan (Deputy Minister of Foreign Affairs/Acting Minister of Foreign Affairs of Thailand) for ASEAN (Bangkok, Thailand, 27 July 1994);
- ASEAN-United States of America Joint Declaration for Cooperation to Combat International Terrorism 2002, signed by Mohamed Bolkiah (Minister of Foreign Affairs of Brunei Darussalam) for ASEAN (Bandar Seri Begawan, Brunei, 2002);
- ASEAN-Canada Joint Declaration for Cooperation to Combat International Terrorism, signed by Dato' Seri Syed Hamid Albar (Minister of Foreign Affairs of Malaysia, Chairman of the 39th ASEAN Standing Committee) for ASEAN (KL, Malaysia, 28 July 2006);
- MOU between ASEAN and the Government of Australia on the 2nd phase of the ASEAN-Australia Development Cooperation Program (AADCP) II 2009, signed by H.E.

[6] Art. 42 ASEAN Charter.

Mr. Kasit Piromya (Minister of Foreign Affairs of the Kingdom of Thailand) for ASEAN (Phuket, Thailand, 23 July 2009).

It is in this way that the Charter invests a member with a specific role in the conduct of external relations, representing ASEAN as a whole.

4.3 Contours of external powers

What matters most with regard to ASEAN external relations is the treaty-making power of ASEAN as an IO. Prior to the ASEAN Charter, the typical practice was to allow the ASEAN Secretariat to conclude non-sensitive agreements on behalf of ASEAN.[7] The general practice in relation to binding international agreements between ASEAN and third parties was – and to the largest degree still is – that all ASEAN Member States sign these agreements. According to widespread belief prior to the Charter, ASEAN as an independent legal person could not do so.[8] That is, ASEAN agreements were concluded in the name of individual ASEAN members and not by ASEAN as an IO. They were concluded only as plurilateral

[7] Report of the Eminent Persons Group on the ASEAN Charter (EPG Report, 2006), available at www.aseansec.org/19247.pdf, at 37. For example, an MOU between ASEAN states and China relating to cultural cooperation was signed by the Secretary-General on behalf of ASEAN and by a Chinese representative on 3 August 2005: www.aseansec.org/17842.htm. See Seah, 'The ASEAN Charter', 204.

[8] S. Tiwari (ed.), *Life after the Charter* (Singapore: Institute of SEA Studies, 2009).

agreements in the way and with the effects discussed in Chapter 6.

Now the ASEAN Charter explicitly provides that ASEAN has legal personality (Article 3). But as Simon Chesterman notes, 'the fact that ASEAN now claims international legal personality in the Charter does not mean it lacked it previously nor that it now possesses it in any meaningful way.'[9] ASEAN's legal personality is now also supported by the 2009 *Agreement on the Privileges and Immunities of the Association of Southeast Asian Nations.*[10] On the face of it, however, ASEAN's legal personality is complemented by few express powers in relation to the conduct of external relations.

Under the Charter, ASEAN has been granted specific, albeit limited powers. Article 41 provides generally that 'ASEAN shall develop friendly relations and mutually beneficial dialogue, cooperation and partnerships with countries and sub-regional, regional and international organisations and institutions.' (Para 1). It shall furthermore 'be the primary driving force in regional arrangements that it initiates and maintain its centrality in regional cooperation and community building'. (Para 3). All this suggests, at the very least, that there is a role for ASEAN to play in external relations.

More specifically, Article 41(7) provides that ASEAN may conduct external relations on behalf of ASEAN through concluding agreements with third party countries or international organizations. In order to do so it needs to follow procedures to be prescribed by the ASEAN Coordinating Council (comprising Foreign Ministers) in consultation with

---

[9] Chesterman, 'Does ASEAN Exist?'.   [10] See in particular Art. 2.

the ASEAN Community Councils (composing senior officers).[11] Furthermore, Article 11(2)(d) empowers the Secretary-General to 'present the views of ASEAN and participate in meetings with external parties in accordance with approved policy guidelines and mandate given to the Secretary-General'. The 2009 *Agreement on the Privileges and Immunities of the Association of Southeast Asian Nations* also states that in the exercise of its 'capacities under international law, including the power to conclude agreements under Article 41(7) of the ASEAN Charter, ASEAN shall act through its representatives authorized by the Member States' Article 2(2).

In addition, the secretariat plays a role in the relationship of ASEAN with so-called 'entities associated with ASEAN' (Article 16 ASEAN Charter). Such entities are listed in Annexx' 2 and include a whole host of bodies such as the Inter-Parliamentary Assembly (IPA), business organisations such as the ASEAN Automotive Federation (AAF), and civil society organisations such as the ASEAN Council of Teachers (ACT), just to name a few examples. The list of associated entities may, according to Article 16 (3), be 'updated by the Secretary-General of ASEAN upon the recommendation of the Committee of Permanent Representatives without recourse to the provision on Amendments under this Charter'. For the conduct of external relations, this has not proven to be of further significance.

---

[11] This does not extend to the capacity of ASEAN to act on behalf of ASEAN, unlike the power of the European Union Commission to act for the Union within the realm of its competence (Arts. 133, 300 European Community Treaty).

With respect to external relations specifically, it is important to note that neither the ASEAN Charter nor the Agreement on the Establishment of the ASEAN Secretariat and its protocols specify that the ASEAN Secretary-General has the power or the mandate to enter into treaty negotiations or to conclude treaties on behalf of ASEAN as an IO, let alone on behalf of the ASEAN Member States. This observation could put a quick end to any further examination of external powers. However, there are a set of provisions that do suggest that the ASEAN Secretary-General does have a role in representing ASEAN externally and that he or she may conclude Memoranda of Understanding (MOUs) and other forms of cooperative agreements. As already indicated above, the ASG has on occasion already done so.

Article 11(2)(a) ASEAN Charter specifies the general framework for such practice in the conduct also of external relations. It provides that the ASG shall 'carry out the duties and responsibilities of this high office in accordance with the provisions of this Charter and relevant ASEAN instruments, protocols and established practices'. Under the Agreement on the Establishment of the ASEAN Secretariat 1976[12] the ASEAN Secretary-General is the 'representative of ASEAN on all matters, in the absence of any decision to the contrary ...'. In other words, the Secretary-General can represent ASEAN unless otherwise restricted by the Chairman of the Standing Committee.

---

[12] As amended by the Protocol Amending the Agreement on the Establishment of the ASEAN Secretariat, Manila, Philippines, 22 July 1992.

In past practice, the ASG has represented ASEAN in signing MOUs and declarations. It has done so variously on behalf of the 'ASEAN Secretariat', 'ASEAN' and 'Government of Member States of ASEAN'. For example, Ong Keng Yong, then Secretary General of ASEAN, signed the already mentioned MOU between ASEAN and the People's Republic of China (PRC) on Cooperation in the Field of Non-Traditional Security Issues (2004) 'for ASEAN'. Conversely, he signed the MOU between ASEAN and PRC on transport cooperation of the same year 'for the Governments of the Member Countries of the ASEAN'. It needs to be teased out what the differences between these forms of commitment are, if any.

The following is a list of a range of agreements, typically MOUs, signed by the Secretary-General, as opposed to the ten Member States:

Signed on behalf of 'ASEAN Secretariat':

1. MOU between ASEAN Secretariat and Ministry of Agriculture of the PRC on Agricultural Cooperation 2002, signed by H.E. Mr. Rodolfo C. Severino Jr. (Secretary-General of ASEAN);

2. MOU between the ASEAN Secretariat and the Ministry of Agriculture of the PRC on Agricultural Cooperation 2007, signed by Ong Keng Yong (Secretary-General of ASEAN) for the Governments of ASEAN Member Countries;

3. MOU between the ASEAN Secretariat and the UN Office on Drugs and Crimes, on Drug Control and Crime Prevention Cooperation, signed by Ong Keng Yong (Secretary-General of ASEAN) for the ASEAN Secretariat;

4. MOU between the ASEAN Secretariat and Shanghai Cooperation Organization (SCO) Secretariat, signed by Ong Keng Yong (Secretary-General) for ASEAN Secretariat;

5. Cooperation Agreement between the Association of Southeast Asian Nations (ASEAN) Secretariat and the International Labour Office 2007, signed by Ong Keng Yong (Secretary-General of ASEAN) for ASEAN Secretariat;

6. MOU between the ASEAN Secretariat and the Secretariat-General of the Cooperation Council for the Arab States of the Gulf 2009, signed by Dr Surin Pitsuwan (Secretary-General of ASEAN) for ASEAN Secretariat;

7. MOU for Administrative Arrangements between the Association of Southeast Asian Nations Secretariat and Asian Development Bank 2006, signed by Ong Keng Yong (Secretary-General of ASEAN);

8. MOU between the ASEAN Secretariat and ESCAP Secretariat 2002, signed by Mr. Rodolfo C. Severino Jr. (Secretary-General of ASEAN) for ASEAN Secretariat.

Signed on behalf of 'ASEAN':

1. MOU between ASEAN and PRC on Cooperation in the Field of Non-Traditional Security Issues 2004, signed by Ong Keng Yong (Secretary-General of ASEAN) for ASEAN;

2. MOU between ASEAN and Government of PRC on Strengthening Sanitary and Phytosanitary Cooperation 2007, signed by Ong Keng Yong (Secretary-General of ASEAN) for ASEAN;

3. MOU between ASEAN and PRC on Cooperation in the Field of Non-Traditional Security Issues 2009, signed by Dr Surin Pitsuwan (Secretary-General of ASEAN) for ASEAN;

4. Agreement between the Government of Indonesia and ASEAN relating to the privileges and immunities of the ASEAN Secretariat 1979, signed by Datuk Ali Bin Abdullah (Secretary-General of ASEAN) for ASEAN;

5. MOU between ASEAN and UN on ASEAN-UN Cooperation 2007, signed by Ong Keng Yong (Secretary-General of ASEAN) for ASEAN;

6. Agreement of Co-operation between the ASEAN and the UNESCO 1998, signed by Rodolfo C. Severino Jr. (Secretary-General) for ASEAN.

Signed on behalf of 'Governments of Member States of ASEAN':

1. MOU between ASEAN and PRC on Transport Cooperation 2004, signed by Ong Keng Yong (Secretary-General of ASEAN) for the Governments of the Member Countries of the ASEAN;

2. MOU between the ASEAN Secretariat and the Ministry of Agriculture of the PRC on Agricultural Cooperation 2007, signed by Ong Keng Yong (Secretary-General of ASEAN) for the Governments of ASEAN Member Countries.

The overview of this practice invites a number of observations. First, the fact that the ASEAN Secretary-General (ASG) acts on behalf of the governments of Member States seems remarkable. On a first glimpse, it could suggest that the ASG enters into agreements that bind the Member States. But, second, without exception such external agreements, typically under the name of 'Memoranda of Understanding', lean towards the soft and 'uncommitted' end of the spectrum of legal obligations in the sense that they are usually hortatory in character. They support very loose forms of cooperation and do not create hard obligations. The 2004 MOU with the PRC on transport cooperation, for example, sets out the objective of cooperation in areas of maritime safety and security (Article II:3), and air transport (Article II:4). It is noteworthy that the issues addressed come within the purview of the Member States: they administer maritime and air transport. When it comes to the implementation of the MOU, Article III gives the ASEAN Secretariat a coordinating and management function to oversee projects carried out on the basis of the MOU.

Overall then, the ASEAN Charter and related instruments, such as the Agreement on Privileges and Immunities, give different actors – above all the ASG, the Secretariat, and the ASEAN host state – roles in external relations. Those roles, however, are not clearly circumscribed and are often times expressed as potentialities, contingent on further processes of authorisation. Could it thus be that the express external powers are complemented by implied powers?

4.4 Implied external powers?

There is room for development in this field of external powers of ASEAN as an IO. From the perspective of international law, the principle of explicitly conferred powers is complemented by the doctrine of implied powers. This doctrine takes different forms. In one version, it weighs in on the interpretative process and is hardly distinguishable from the doctrine of *effet utile*. It demands that power-conferring provisions are interpreted so that their effect is guaranteed to the fullest degree possible.[13] In this vein, an implied power may be found to exist by virtue of another explicit power unless there are other explicit textual provisions that contradict such a finding.[14] The *effet utile* doctrine has been very prominent in the case law of the European Court of Justice, especially when it comes to the EU's external relations powers. In the classic *Fédéchar* case of 1955 – even before the ECJ (now CJEU) claimed that the European legal order was autonomous from international law – it held that 'the rules laid down by an international treaty or a law presuppose the rules without which that treaty or law would have no meaning or could not be reasonably and usefully applied.'[15]

On another occasion, the ECJ held that the community's power to enter into external agreements not only arises from express provisions on external competences in the constitutive treaty, but also from other provisions to the extent that external action is necessary to meet the objectives of

---

[13] See in further detail J. Klabbers, *An Introduction to International Institutional Law* (Cambridge: Cambridge University Press, 2002) 67–75.

[14] See already Permanent Court of International Justice, *Interpretation of the Greco-Turkish Agreement of December 1st 1926*, [1928] PCIJ, Series B, no. 16, 20.

[15] Case 8/55. Fédération Charbonnière de *Belgique v High Authority* [1956] ECR 292, 299.

those provisions.[16] The court refined this doctrine and furthermore shaped a principle of parallelism according to which the union is competent to enter into international agreements provided that it parallels *internal* competences related to specific objectives and international agreements which are necessary to achieve such objectives.[17]

According to a second, yet more expansive version, the implied powers doctrine may be read so as to suggest that an organisation may be presumed to have those competences which are necessary for it to effectively carry out its functions and to pursue its objectives. It is in this form that the doctrine of implied powers has perhaps found its most famous expression in the International Court of Justice's Advisory Opinion on *Reparation for Injuries*, where the court held that:

> the Organization must be deemed to have those powers which, though not expressly provided in the Charter, are conferred upon it by necessary implication as being essential to the performance of its duties.[18]

In this variation, implied powers do not need to be explicitly linked to any express power, but they more loosely connect to the objectives and purposes of the organisation – to the 'performance of its duties'. This is certainly a highly flexible standard. It is this understanding of the implied power

---

[16] Case 22/70, *ERTA* [1971] ECR 263 paras 16 and 28; Opinion 1/76 [1977] ECR 741, paras 3–4.

[17] Klabbers, *An Introduction*, 69.

[18] *Reparation for Injuries Suffered in the Service of United Nations*, Advisory Opinion, [1949] ICJ Reports 174, 182.

doctrine that has largely prevailed and it is this variation that has gained strength in the process of European integration.

When it comes to ASEAN, a number of preconditions underlying any such kind of reasoning are different. Notably, the cases in which the ECJ employed the doctrine of implied powers and the principle of parallelism between internal and external competences are connected to fields in which the EU had clear internal legislative (regulatory) competences. In comparison, ASEAN Member States have not vested ASEAN with any comparable powers. It would appear that inferring external treaty-making competences by implication would seem rather far-fetched. On the other hand, there are variations of the implied powers doctrine that would be suitable also in the ASEAN context, for example, in connection to the *express* powers of Article 41(7) ASEAN Charter.

4.5 Who is bound? The effect on Member States

In order to further understand the effects of external agreements that ASEAN enters into as an IO it is necessary to gain clarity on the question as to who is bound. On a preliminary note it is clear that, when an organ of the organisation, that is, the ASEAN Secretary-General concludes an agreement, it binds the IO. The general position of international law on this issue was affirmed by the International Court of Justice in the *Effect of Awards* case in which it first added further weight to the implied powers doctrine by finding that the UN General Assembly (GA) had the power to create the UN Administrative Tribunal (UNAT) even if such power was not listed in the UN Charter: 'the capacity to do this arises by necessary intendment out of the Charter'.[19] It then found that awards rendered by UNAT, set up by the GA, in effect bind the UN as a whole, and not just the GA or the Secretariat.[20] This part of the opinion is taken to support the general view of international law that agreements entered into by organs of the organisation will bind the organisation as a whole.[21]

In the European Union, the effect of external agreements on the internal relations has been spelled out by Article 216 of the Treaty on the Functioning of the European Union (TFEU), which provides that '[a]greements concluded by the Union are binding upon the institutions of the Union'. Thus, while the traditional opinion of international law is that a treaty binds the international organisation as a whole, Article 216 extends external obligations onto all organs and thus speaks in this way on the internal effects. In earlier case law preceding the latest treaty reforms, the commission had argued that an agreement that it concluded with the US Department of Justice to cooperate in antitrust affairs was only binding on itself, not on the community as a whole. The ECJ rejected that argument stating that international law knows of no such administrative agreements. Instead, agreements that the Commission entered into are binding on the Community as a whole.[22]

[19] *Effect of awards of compensation made by the United Nations Administrative Tribunal*, Advisory Opinion, [1954] ICJ Reports 47, 57
[20] *Ibid.*, at 58–59 and 87.   [21] See Klabbers, *An Introduction*, 288.
[22] Case C-327/91 *France v Commission* [1994] ECR I-3641, paras 24–25.

A different question concerns the effect of the IO's external agreements on the position of Member States. Article 216 TFEU is also clear on this as it reads in full that '[a]greements concluded by the Union are binding upon the institutions of the Union *and on its Member States*' (emphasis added). No similar provision can be found in ASEAN instruments.

As a matter of general international law, the effect of agreements concluded by an IO on Member States is contested. The International Law Commission, when deliberating upon the 1986 Vienna Convention on the Law of Treaties between States and International Organizations or between International Organizations, could not produce a rule on this issue. A draft Article 36*bis* was included at one point, which spoke precisely to the '[e]ffects of a treaty to which an international organization is party with respect to States members of that organization'. It read in its early formulation:

> 1. A treaty concluded by an international organization gives rise directly for States members of an international organization to rights and obligations in respect of other parties to that treaty if the constituent instrument of that organization expressly gives such effects to the treaty.

> 2. When, on account of the subject-matter of a treaty concluded by an international organization and the assignment of areas of competence involved in that subject-matter between the organization and its Member States, it appears that such was indeed the intention of the parties to that treaty, the treaty gives rise for a Member State to: (i) rights, which the Member State is presumed to

accept, in the absence of any indication of intention to the contrary; (ii) obligations when the Member State accepts them, even implicitly.

The first paragraph takes care of the constellations in which the treaty setting up the IO clearly states that the IO's external agreements are binding on Member States, as is the case for the European Union. The Union is unique in being the only institution beyond the state that contains such a provision and which, in fact, distinguishes itself through this and through other features as a *supra*-national organisation. Article 38*bis* was thus criticised as being modeled to take account of the European Economic Community alone.[23] The second paragraph, slightly convoluted, refers to a scenario in which a treaty by an international organisation can create rights and obligations for Member States provided that three conditions are met: (i) the treaty created rights or obligations for Member States; (ii) the members unanimously agreed on becoming bound by such a treaty; (iii) the other party or parties to the treaty are notified of the fact that Member States will also be bound.[24]

Whereas the first paragraph was clear and stated what is at least now obvious, the second paragraph gave rise

---

[23] C. Brölmann, *The Institutional Veil in Public International Law: International Law and the Law of Treaties* (Portland, OR: Hart, 2007) 214.

[24] C. Brölmann, 'The 1986 Vienna Convention on the Law of Treaties: The history of Draft Article 36bis', in J. Klabbers and R. Lefeber (eds.), *Essays on the Law of Treaties: A collection of Essays in Honour of Bert Vierdag* (The Hague: Martinus Nijhoff, 1998) 121–140; Klabbers, *An Introduction*, 261.

to protracted controversies that simply could not escape the persistent riddle: either Member States were not parties and were thus not bound (other than, possibly, though a provision to that effect within the constituent instrument of the organisation), or they were parties, in which case the third party concluded a treaty with both the IO *and* its members. The latter scenario corresponds to the experience of mixed agreements in the European context.[25] States feared to become bound without their clear consent, and in the end, Article *38bis* was deleted completely. Thus, even this cautious draft article was ultimately rejected because it did not pay sufficient respect to the fundamental tenet that states cannot be bound without their express consent – as a matter of principle then, neither could they be bound by acts of the organisation that they created.

From the perspective of general international law, there seems to be no way out of this riddle: either the will of the organisation is reduced to nothing more than the sum of the will of each state party (aggregative model), or the distinct legal personality of the IO is taken seriously with a distinct will of its own, in which case an argument that its Member States would also be bound by the agreements it concludes would contradict the idea that only states make the law that bind them. The latter view would contradict the general principle that treaties cannot create rights or obligations for third parties. The way out of this quandary in the context of European integration has been a conferral of competence with

---

[25] See Section 7.1 on 'An (ill-)fitting Comparison: Mixed Agreements'.

a concomitant provision that Member States are bound by the Community's external action (i.e. Article 216 TFEU).

Agreements entered into by the Community can even create direct effect in the Member States.[26] Notably, however, Member States are bound by way of their commitment made in the treaties of the European Union, not by the international agreement to which they are not party. From the perspective of international law, an international agreement by an international or supranational organisation and a third party cannot bind members of the organisation. If Member States have also expressed their consent, as happens in case of mixed agreements (on that see Chapter 7), then they are also to be considered parties to the agreement.

4.6 Members' concurrent and subsidiary responsibility or indirect liability

One important question remains. Even if members are generally not bound by agreements that an IO enters into, could they be responsible for the IO's failure to live up to its obligations and commitments? It is accepted that an IO with legal personality has the capacity to bear rights and duties, and, as a corollary, can also be internationally responsible.[27] The International Law Commission's (ILC) Articles on the Responsibility of International Organizations now spells out the most authoritative, though contested, framework in this

---

[26] Case 104/81 *Kupferberg* [1982] ECR 3641.
[27] *Reparation for Injuries Suffered in the Service of United Nations,* Advisory Opinion, [1949] ICJ Reports 174, 179.

regard.[28] But with a view to the internal effects of the external agreements that ASEAN concludes as an IO, under which conditions could the Member States of ASEAN possibly be responsible or liable?

The classic case of the *International Tin Council* (ITC) comes to mind.[29] The ITC was created in 1956 as an IO, whose statutory framework was repeatedly adjusted, most lately with the Sixth International Tin Agreement (ITA) of 1982. Twenty-three states and the European Economic Community were parties to the ITA and, according to Article 16 ITA, the ITC was vested with legal personality.[30] Members included the main producers and purchasers of tin, who shared an interest in relatively stable prices and stable supply. They thus tasked the ITC with intervening in the global tin market (buying tin and building up a stock when prices were low and selling tin when prices were high). Similar mechanisms were set up in the markets for other

---

[28] International Law Commission, 'Draft Articles on the Responsibility of International Organizations, with Commentaries', 63rd session, 2011, available at http://legal.un.org/ilc/texts/instruments/english/commentaries/9_11_2011.pdf.

[29] See generally, M. Hartwig, *Die Haftung der Mitgliedstaaten für Internationale Organisationen* (Heidelberg: Springer, 1993); I. Pernice, 'Die Haftung internationaler Organisationen und ihrer Mitglieder, dargestellt am "Fall" des internationalen Zinnrates' (1988) 26 *Archiv des Völkerrechts* 406–433; C.F. Amerasinghe, 'Liability to Third Parties of Member States of International Organizations: Practice, Principle and Judicial Precedent' (1991) 85 *American Journal of International Law* 259–280.

[30] For an overview see M. Hartwig, 'The International Tin Council (ITC)', in R. Wolfrum (ed.), *Max Planck Encyclopedia of Public International Law* (Oxford: Oxford University Press, 2011).

commodities. The ITC was further authorised to conclude a headquarters agreement, which it did conclude in 1972 with the United Kingdom (its headquarters was in London). It is interesting to note that the ITC was also authorised to enter into cooperation agreements with the UN, specialized agencies, and other organisations (Article 25 ITA).[31] What triggered the case as one of possible Member State liability was that, with continuously falling tin prices in the 1980s, the ITC piled up purchasing commitments that it eventually could no longer meet. It went bankrupt with a debt of £900 million.[32]

Creditors then sought repayment of their loans, not only from the ITC, which lacked assets, but also from the members. One of the obvious question that arose was whether members could be held liable for the actions of the ITC. Relevant proceedings were initiated before English courts, where this question was closely linked with questions of the immunity of the ITC and the applicability of international law. In one salient case, *Maclaine Watson & Co Ltd v Department of Trade and Industry and Others*, the plaintiffs advanced the arguments that, first, the ITC was not in fact vested with a legal personality of its own and members were thus directly liable; second, even if the ITC had a legal personality of its own, members bore a concurrent or secondary

---

[31] *Ibid.* para 1.
[32] *Ibid.* para 7. For a concise summary of the background see also R. Sadurska and C. M. Chinkin, 'The Collapse of the International Tin Council: A Case of State Responsibility?' (1990) 30 *Virginia Journal of International Law* 845–890 at 849–850.

liability; third and finally, the ITC functioned merely as an agent under the control of members.[33]

The Court of Appeal rejected the first argument without much ado. The parliamentary statute, which incorporated the headquarters agreement, provided that the ITC is a body corporate under English law and was thus a distinct entity separate from its members, and immune from suit.[34] Two Lord Justices further supported this finding with the argument that the ICT qualifies as an IO, as it has the capacity to conclude international treaties such as a headquarters agreement.

With regard to the question of concurrent or secondary liability of members for the acts of the IO, the three judges were clearly split. One Lord Justice found that there is no rule to such effect in international law. Another judge was of the contrary opinion that the parties did have the intention of creating a rule in the ITA according to which they would be jointly and severally liable. The third judge, however, argued that international law could not be applied to this question as the law was not incorporated within the domestic legal order. Municipal law knows no such liability for members. In conclusion, the plaintiff's second argument was rejected as well.[35]

---

[33] *Maclaine Watson & Co Ltd v Department of Trade and Industry and Others* 26 October 1989, House of Lords, 81 ILR 670.

[34] See Headquarters Agreement Arts. 6, 23, 24. *Maclaine Watson & Co Ltd v Department of Trade and Industry, and JH Rayner (Mincing Lane) Ltd v Department of Trade and Industry and Others, and Related Appeals,* United Kingdom Court of Appeal (27 April 1988) 80 ILR 49.

[35] *Ibid.*

Finally, the judges did not consider that the members exerted such control over the organisation such that it could be considered to be merely acting as an agent. This last point turned on the decision-making provisions and the legal relationship between the organisation and its members. The ITC's main organ was the Council, which generally decided by a simple majority of the group of producer countries and consumer countries (Article 15(1) ITA). Even if some decisions required a two-thirds majority, these provisions set up an organisation with a distinct will-formation process that could not be reduced to the aggregate will and control of members. The view that the ITC acted as an agent of the members who would therefore be liable was thus also dismissed.[36]

Finally, when the case was appealed, the House of Lords added little to the arguments as it found inter-national law to be non-applicable to this issue.[37] It did however state, *obiter dictum*, that there was no evidence for an international rule that would hold members second-arily or concurrently liable for an organisation's debt, unless they provided otherwise.[38] The ITA did not contain

---

[36] *Ibid.*

[37] See further A. Reinisch, *International Organizations Before National Courts* (Cambridge: Cambridge University Press, 2000) 119–120.

[38] *JH Rayner (Mincing Lane) Ltd v Department of Trade and Industry and Others and Related Appeals, and Maclaine Watson & Co Ltd v Department of Trade and Industry, and Maclaine Watson & Co Ltd v International Tin Council*, United Kingdom House of Lords (26 October 1989) 81 ILR 670.

any provision on members' liability for acts of the organisation.[39]

The inapplicability of relevant international law before the domestic courts of the United Kingdom prevented further input and possibly, clarification on the question of members' liability. The case of the ITC did however fuel scholarly debate and pushed the topic onto the agenda of the *Institut de droit international* and the International Law Commission (ILC).[40] The *Institut* concluded after much debate in 1994 that 'there is no general rule of international law whereby Member States are, due solely to their membership, liable concurrently or subsidiarily, for the obligations of an international organization of which they are members.'[41] The only conditions under which a Member State could be liable are that (i) the statute or the rules of the organisation say so; (ii) a general principle of international law such as

---

[39] Further see on this issue M. Hartwig, 'International Organizations or Institutions, Responsibility and Liability', in R. Wolfrum (ed.), *Max Planck Encyclopedia of Public International Law* (Oxford: Oxford University Press, 2011)

[40] See, among others, M. Herdegen, 'The Insolvency of International Organizations and the Legal Position of Creditors: Some Observations in the Light of the International Tin Council Crisis' (1988) 35 *Netherlands International Law Review* 135–144; for an overview see C. Ryngaert and H. Buchanan, 'Member State Responsibility for the Acts of International Organizations' (2011) 7 *Utrecht Law Review* 131–146 at 136–138.

[41] Art. 6, Institut de Droit International, 'The Legal Consequences for Member States of the Non-fulfillment by International Organizations of their Obligations toward Third Parties' 1995, available at www.idi-iil.org/idiE/resolutionsE/1995_lis_02_en.pdf.

acquiescence or abuse of right provides for their liability; (iii) the organisation acted as an agent of the state.[42]

The relevant work of the ILC on the issue has culminated in the Articles on the Responsibility of International Organizations (ARIO).[43] They also do not readily lend support to the view that members could be liable for acts of the international organisation solely by virtue of their membership. Part V details explicitly with when a state may be held responsible for the conduct of an international organisation. It includes scenarios in which a state aids or assists an IO in the commission of the wrongful act (Article 58), directs or controls the IO (Article 59), or coerces an IO (Article 60). In those cases, clearly, the act of the state itself is wrongful, possibly in addition to the act of the IO.[44] In those cases, and in cases in which a state or a state organ acts as an agent of an IO or is placed at the disposal of an IO (Article 7 ARIO), the scenario may be one of shared responsibility between states and the IO. Both the acts of states and the IO would be individually wrongful and questions would pertain to the way in which their responsibility is shared, or the ways in which conduct is attributable to

[42] *Ibid.*, Art. 5.
[43] International Law Commission, 'Draft Articles on the Responsibility of International Organizations, with Commentaries', 63rd session, 2011, available at http://legal.un.org/ilc/texts/instruments/english/commentaries/9_11_2011.pdf.
[44] That much follows from the formulation of the articles, which state explicitly that 'a state ... is internationally responsible' if it aids, assists, directs, controls or coerces an international organization in the commission of an internationally wrongful act (subject to further conditions).

multiple actors.[45] The constellations are thus distinct from holding members responsible for a wrongful act of the IO. Such would be the situation envisaged of Article 62 and, arguably, of Article 61.

According to Article 62, a Member State is responsible for an internationally wrongful act of the organisation only if (i) it has accepted the responsibility or (ii) it has led the injured party to rely on its responsibility. The ILC's commentary on that article continues to state in the form of a general rule that 'membership does not as such entail for Member States' international responsibility when the organization commits an internationally wrongful act.'[46] A rule to the contrary – that is, providing for the possibility of members' responsibility for wrongful acts of the IO – is frequently argued to undermine the autonomy of the IO. The causal and factual assumptions embedded in this reasoning have, however, been plausibly questioned.[47]

---

[45] On these issues see A. Nollkaemper and D. Jacobs, 'Shared Responsibility in International Law: A Conceptual Framework' (2013) 34 *Michigan Journal of International Law* 359–438; F. Messineo, 'Multiple Attribution of Conduct', in A. Nollkaemper and I. Plakokefalos (eds.), *Principles of Shared Responsibility* (Cambridge: Cambridge University Press, 2014).

[46] International Law Commission, 'Draft Articles on the Responsibility of International Organizations, with Commentaries', 63rd session, 2011, 96. Available at http://legal.un.org/ilc/texts/instruments/english/commentaries/9_11_2011.pdf.

[47] A. Stumer, 'Liability of Member States for Acts of International Organizations: Reconsidering the Policy Objections' (2007) 48 *Harvard International Law Journal* 553–580.

Article 61 pertains to cases in which a member is responsible because it has circumvented its own obligations through the IO. This article might be taken to pierce the corporate veil of the organisation. That is not persuasive, however, because this article, like Articles 58–60, is better understood as dealing with the responsibility of the Member States for their own individually wrongful acts, not for acts of the organisation. Para 2 of Article 61 supports this by clarifying that the article applies regardless of whether the act of the organisation is internationally wrongful or not. What is at issue is the act of Member States. The jurisprudence on which the ILC bases this article, decidedly as a progressive development of the law, also concerns constellations where members were held responsible. The European Court of Human Rights (ECtHR), for instance, stated clearly that a member of an IO could itself be found responsible if it did not take necessary measures to ensure that the IO would not violate the European Convention of Human Rights.[48] The reasoning of the ECtHR here relates to the responsibility of the Member States for not having prevented acts of the IO, not to any responsibility for the acts of the IO. The Member State's own omission gives rise to responsibility.[49] The point is that a member must

---

[48] *Bosphorus v Ireland* [ECtHR] Reports 2005-VI 107, para 155; *Waite and Kennedy v Germany* [ECtHR] Reports 1999-I 393, para 67.

[49] See in further detail O. Murray, 'Piercing the Corporate Veil: The Responsibility of Member States of an International Organization' (2011) 8 *International Organizations Law Review* 291–347.

not be allowed to circumvent its own obligations by setting up or acting through an IO.[50]

Article 61 may yet be pushed further, as Oddette Murray argues, to possibly extend to how Member States exercise their discretion in taking part in the operation of the IO, especially through voting.[51] While voting is a discretionary and a 'political' exercise, this does not necessarily put voting beyond the reach of legal regulation. In Murray's view, Article 61 specifies a general prohibition of abuse of right, which extends precisely to areas of political discretion.[52] According to this line of reasoning, members might possibly be held responsible for their votes, in parallel to the responsibility of the IO, but not for acts of the IO.

The question that still remains is what members might be required to do in cases where the IO acts wrongfully and might, as in the case of the International Tin Council, be unable to meet its obligations. In that exemplary case,

---

[50] Hartwig, 'International Organizations or Institutions, Responsibility and Liability', para 25; in detail see J. d'Aspremont, 'Abuse of the Legal Personality of International Organizations and the Responsibility of Member States' (2007) 4 *International Organization Law Review* 91–119; K. E. Boon, 'New Directions in Responsibility: Assessing the International Law Commission's Draft Articles on the Responsibility of International Organizations' (2011) 37 *Yale Journal of International Law* 1–10.

[51] See Murray, 'Piercing the Corporate Veil'.

[52] *Ibid.* 299–300 and 339; also with reference to Art. 5(b) of the 1995 Resolution of the *Institut de Droit International*: 'In particular circumstances, members of an international organization may be liable for its obligations in accordance with a relevant general principle of international law, such as acquiescence or the abuse of rights.'

members certainly did not accept responsibility, nor did they in any way lead third parties to rely on their responsibility. It is questionable that they themselves acted wrongfully in the sense of Article 61 ARIO. In those cases, members' obligation to provide adequate financing may possibly be reconsidered.

In this regard, Article 40(2) of the ARIO provides that members of an organisation that has committed an internationally wrongful act 'shall take all the appropriate measures that may be required by the rules of the organization in order to enable the organisation to fulfill its obligations under this Chapter [on reparation for injury]'. As the ILC Commentary explains further, this article views members' responsibility as possibly stemming from the rules of the organisation. It does not claim that there is a general rule of international law on that matter, nor does it necessarily consider the rules of the organisation as international law.[53] So, 'breaches of obligations under the rules of the organisation are not always breaches of obligations under international law'.[54]

At the same time, however, Article 32 of the ARIO provides that a 'responsible international organization may not rely on its rules as justification for failure to comply with its obligations under this part'. That provision falls within the part on the 'content of the international responsibility of an international organization', which also includes Article 40;

---

[53] International Law Commission, 'Draft Articles on the Responsibility of International Organizations, with Commentaries', 63rd session, 2011, 33. Available at http://legal.un.org/ilc/texts/instruments/english/commentaries/9_11_2011.pdf
[54] *Ibid.*

Article 31, for instance, provides for the organisation's 'obligation to make full reparation for the injury caused by the internationally wrongful act'. It might thus be argued that the failure of the rules of the organisation to require members to take those measures (i.e. financial contributions), which are adequate to meet its obligations to pay reparations for injuries, also does not get the organisation or its member states off the hook. In particular, members might not be in a position to avoid bearing financial burdens if they are under an obligation to ensure the organisation's effective functioning and such functioning includes the provision of necessary financial resources.[55] Judge Fitzmaurice recognised as much in his separate opinion in *Certain Expenses of the United Nations*:

> Without finance, the Organization could not perform its duties. Therefore, even in the absence of Article 17, paragraph 2 [Charter of the United Nations], a general obligation for Member States collectively to finance the Organization would have to be read into the Charter, on the basis of the same principle as the Court applied in the Injuries to United Nations Servants case, namely 'by necessary implication as being essential to the performance of its [the Organization's] duties'.[56]

[55] On this issue see C. Ahlborn, 'The Rules of International Organizations and the Law of International Responsibility' (2011) 8 *International Organizations Law Review* 397–482 at 469.

[56] *Certain Expenses of the United Nations (Article 17, paragraph 2, of the Charter)*, Separate Opinion of Judge Sir Gerald Fitzmaurice, [1962] ICJ Reports 198, 208, referring to *Reparation for Injuries Suffered in the Service of United Nations*, Advisory Opinion, [1949] ICJ Reports 174, 182. See Ahlborn, 'The Rules of International Organizations', 469.

Article 17(2) UN Charter provides that '[t]he expenses of the Organization shall be borne by the members as apportioned by the General Assembly.' The question in *Certain Expenses* was whether the costs of peacekeeping operations could be considered costs of the organisation, and the International Court of Justice answered in the affirmative.[57] What Judge Fritzmaurice suggests is that members are under a general obligation to ensure the organisation's effective functioning and to thus provide financing even in the absence of Article 17(2). In her discussion of member's responsibility, Christiane Ahlborn builds on this logic and applies it to cases of reparations for injuries from organizations' wrongful acts:

> [I]t could be suggested that the termination of the international organization – due to a lack of resources or another failure on the part of its member States – will result in the collective responsibility of the contracting parties to its constituent instruments, so as to avoid a legal vacuum for injured third parties.[58]

In her nuanced assessment, members would thus ultimately have to provide the funding for an IO to meet the obligations stemming from an international wrongful act, such as the payment of reparations. Given that the organisation itself typically has rather limited resources, the scenario that members' contributions are necessary for the continuous

---

[57] *Certain Expenses of the United Nations (Article 17, paragraph 2, of the Charter)*, Advisory Opinion [1962] ICJ Reports 151.

[58] Ahlborn, 'The Rules of International Organizations', 470. Similarly, J. Klabbers, *An Introduction to International Institutional Law*, 2nd edn. (Cambridge: Cambridge University Press, 2009) 288.

effective functioning of the organisation might not be all that exceptional. Matthias Hartwig adopts the yet more general view that:

> The ICJ decided in the Certain Expenses case of 1962 that the payments of the members must meet all the costs of the international organization. It also includes the expenditures which are due as a consequence of responsibility for a breach of international law. It means that States have to pay the expenditures of the international organization according to the share which has been attributed to them, as far as there is no limitation of their liability as, eg, in the cases of the commodity agreements. In this sense, one can say that the Member States are indirectly liable for the action of the international organization.[59]

Arguably, the internal rules of the organisation could, as few statutes do, expressly limit members' liability.[60] The discussion would then turn to questions of whether members can legally do so and when their establishment of an IO under such conditions might incur their own state responsibility because they abuse rights or try to circumvent their responsibility. That would then be an issue of Article 61.[61] Separate from that consideration, we submit that

---

[59] Hartwig, 'International Organizations or Institutions, Responsibility and Liability', para 33.

[60] See, e.g., Art. II (3) Articles of Agreement of the International Development Association: 'No member shall be liable, by reason of its membership, for obligations of the Association'

[61] On the role of good faith and abuse of rights as underlying principles of the ARIO, see Murray, 'Piercing the Corporate Veil'.

members bear an indirect liability to stem the costs of reparation for IOs' wrongful acts. Underlying these considerations is the policy reason that IOs themselves oftentimes lack the resources to meet their obligations. In that sense, the reasoning connected to Article 40 ('members shall take all the appropriate measures that may be required by the rules of the organization in order to enable the organization to fulfil its obligations under this Chapter [on reparation for injury]') and the logic underlying Article 61 are related. State members should not be allowed to set up an organisation in a way that allows them to escape their own international responsibility or financial liability.

When it comes to ASEAN, the first thing to note is that neither the Charter nor any other instrument limits the liability of members for acts of the organisation. That is not surprising as few agreements other than commodities agreements in fact do so. Given the scope of activities of ASEAN as an IO it is, furthermore, unlikely that it will incur obligations for reparations in relation to third parties. In that sense, the present considerations largely project into the unknown future. However, ASEAN's activities within third countries, and in relation to third parties more generally, could in principle trigger such a scenario.

When it comes to voting patterns, contrary to many other IOs where voting might be weighted (such as in the International Financial Institutions) or where some members have elevated roles (such as in the United Nations Security Council), the decision-making rules of ASEAN pay tribute to the sovereign equality of Member State. The rules do not break with the equal value of each member and further, by default, demand that decisions are taken by consensus.[62] Under these rules, and given the actual power-dynamics within ASEAN, it is unlikely that ASEAN as an IO would come under the control of one or a couple of Member State(s) only. What might be more likely to happen is that a Member State may provoke the international responsibility of ASEAN by obstructing a decision. It could then be asked whether that member might incur international legal responsibility. But that is a question that is only loosely connected to the internal effect of ASEAN external agreements and focused on those limited cases in which a vote would be necessary to prevent an internationally wrongful act of the IO. This thought projects too far into the future to merit further analysis at this point.

[62] See Chapter 2.

Chapter 5

Plurilateral agreements

On the face of it, most ASEAN external agreements present themselves as *plurilateral agreements*. The parties to such agreements are a minimum number, if not all, of ASEAN Member States and any number of third states. In the large majority of cases, the language of ASEAN external agreements is seemingly clear-cut and speaks, for example, of '[a]n agreement between ASEAN Member States and the Republic of Korea (ROK) on Forestry Cooperation'.[1] At times, to meet any remaining doubt, some external agreements specify further. For example, Article 3 Agreement Establishing the ASEAN-Australia-New Zealand Free Trade Area (AANZFTA) provides that '*[p]arties* means the ASEAN Member States, Australia and New Zealand collectively; . . . *[p]arty* means an ASEAN Member State or Australia or New Zealand'. ASEAN as an IO is obviously not a party to the agreement.

The fact that in some instances the ASEAN Secretary-General also signs such agreements is immaterial if such agreements are read as traditional plurilateral agreements. On this reading, varieties of the formula that refers to ASEAN as a collectivity do not detract from the plainly plurilateral nature of the agreements. Where ASEAN is referred to as a collectivity, this may be understood to be an umbrella term or

---

[1] Advancing Forestry Cooperation in International Year of Forest 2011, Bali, Indonesia, 18 November 2011.

shorthand for the individual Member States.[2] This means that it is the governments of the respective ASEAN Member States who conclude the agreement rather than ASEAN as an institutional entity. That they collectively form ASEAN is inconsequential with regard to the nature of the external instrument as a plurilateral agreement. Where the present type of external agreements is concerned, ASEAN as an IO is sidelined. At the most, it provides a forum for treaty making by its Member States, or it serves as a venue for coordination. As plurilateral agreements, the internal effects of ASEAN external agreements are equal to the effects within ASEAN Member States of any other international agreement.

The internal effects of ASEAN external agreements may of course differ in light of the nature of the agreement and in view of the specific obligations that such agreements create for Member States. Salient points to consider include whether agreements require that Member States bring their domestic legislation in conformity, whether the existence of contrary legislation itself triggers state responsibility, whether obligations set out in international agreements are sufficiently precise, or whether complainants can seek redress or relief from international dispute settlement mechanisms.[3] This section

---

[2] For variations of this formula and possible rationalities behind those variations, see the contribution by Cremona, Venesson and Lee, 'The External Agreements of ASEAN'.

[3] The ASEAN Plus Three (APT) agreements with China, Japan, and Korea are noteworthy in this regard, see C.-H. Wu, 'The ASEAN Economic Community under the ASEAN Charter: Its External Economic Relations and Dispute Settlement Mechanism' (2010) 1 *European Yearbook of International Economic Law* 331–357.

continues by articulating a general framework for approaching the internal effects of plurilateral external agreements.

The status that any specific plurilateral external agreements will assume within the domestic legal order depends both on the features of that agreement itself as well as on the internal law of any particular state party. Internal effects are thus a result of the relationship between international and municipal law. Both influence issues of reception, applicability, and hierarchy, for instance. Both will need to be considered in order to see, for example, whether a treaty is self-executing or whether a further act of legislative incorporation is necessary for the treaty to have domestic legal effect.

The very rough and porous categories according to which the municipal law side to that equation is commonly divided are that of dualism and monism. That binary distinction has lost much of its purchase and explanatory power, as we will continue to show. Since it is still influential in the constitutional discourse of ASEAN Member States, we employ it in the following first steps towards understanding international law's international effects. Most ASEAN countries are considered dualist, regardless of whether they stand in a common law or civil law tradition. The Philippines, for example, takes a largely dualist stance and requires that treaties need to satisfy the domestic legal requirements of ratification, except for those international agreements implementing existing agreements, foreign loan agreements and commercial contracts.[4] But at the same time, the Philippines shows

---

[4] J. E. E. Malaya and M. A. Mendoza-Oblena, 'Philippine Treaty Law and Practice' (2010) 35 *Integrated Bar of the Philippines Journal* 1–17, available

openness towards international law, at least what concerns certain human rights instruments.[5] This example already shows the limits of the dualism and monism divide.

This section proceeds by offering terminological and conceptual clarifications on the issue of internal effects (a). After this background is set out, it approaches the internal effect of plurilateral agreements between ASEAN Member States and third states from the view of international law (b) and from the perspective of the constitutional ordering of domestic law (c). Since there is frequently considerable space for interpretative maneuver, it is further helpful to see clearly the different policy considerations involved in matters of internal effect (d).

5.1 Terminology: monism, dualism and (in)direct effects

It is common to distinguish, first of all, *direct* from *indirect* effect. At the same time, the basis upon which to draw such a distinction is not entirely settled. Is the *status* of international law as valid law in domestic contexts, or the *kind of effect* that international law has in domestic settings, the relevant criterion? Issues of what rank international law has (or should assume) within the domestic legal order also arise.

at http://dfa.gov.ph/treaties/ola/Treaty%20Law%20and%20Practice.pdf. Section 21 of the Philippines Constitution (1987) provides that no treaty or international agreement shall be valid and effective unless it has the concurrence of 2/3 Senate members.

[5] D. Desierto, ASEAN ITL Project, Country Report on the Philippines.

When focusing on the status of international law in domestic law from the perspective of municipal law, the received distinction is that between *monist* and *dualist* approaches.[6] A *monist* approach suggests that international law forms part of the valid law within the domestic setting – there is, strictly speaking, only one legal order that transcends all levels of governance.

The *dualist* approach to the status of international law suggests that international law only becomes part of domestic law if it is transposed into the domestic setting by acts of incorporation, whether this is accomplished through legislation, administrative directive, or by other means. The distinction turns on whether and when international law is valid law in the domestic setting; that is, whether and when it can be the basis of a judgment about legality: *directly*, without an act of transformation from the international into the domestic setting; or *indirectly*, only after incorporation.

We will detail later how the explanatory power of both monism and dualism suffers due to two main reasons. First, it turns out that domestic legal orders usually combine elements of both approaches (as the introductory example of the Philippines already showed). Second, the actual workings of international law seem to depend at least as much on

6 See in detail C. Amrhein-Hofmann, *Monismus und Dualismus in den Völkerrechtslehren* (Berlin: Duncker & Humblot, 2003); A. Nollkaemper and J. E. Nijman (eds.), *New Perspectives on the Divide between National and International Law* (Oxford: Oxford University Press, 2007); T. Finegan, 'Neither Dualism nor Monism: Holism and the Relationship between Municipal and International Human Rights Law' (2011) 2 *Transnational Legal Theory* 477–503.

prevalent attitudes of groups of interpreters and on interpretative patterns than on the formal status granted to
international law.[7] For purposes of terminological clarity, it
is important for now to note that the distinction between
direct and indirect effect may first pertain to the *conditions
of validity of international law*; that is, on its *status* in
municipal law.

A second but not unrelated way of distinguishing
direct from indirect effect instead focuses on the kind of effect
that international law has in domestic legal operations. *Direct*
effect would again refer to the fact that international law
forms the basis of a judgment about legality. *Indirect* effects
would include all the other kinds of effects that international
law shows; primarily, this would be through its impact on the
interpretative process.[8]

To illustrate briefly by way of example: it may well be
that an international instrument such as the European Convention on Human Rights (ECHR) does not have direct effect
in a Member State. Such is the case, for instance, in Germany
where the ECHR does not form part of the valid domestic law.
If, however, domestic law is applied, the German Constitutional Court requires that it be interpreted, where relevant, in

---

[7] For the crucial role that domestic courts play in this regard, and for their
relative leeway, see A. Nollkaemper, 'The Duality of Direct Effect of
International Law' (2014) 25 *European Journal of International Law*
105–125.

[8] That these two understandings are not unrelated is visible upon closer
scrutiny because domestic organs give indirect effect to international law
especially where the domestic statute to be applied implements an
international obligation.

light of the ECHR as shaped by the European Courts of Human Rights (ECtHR).[9] The ECHR and the case law of the ECtHR are *indirectly* effective within the German internal legal order. The issue is not whether they need to be transposed to be valid law ('status') but whether they can have effects other than forming the basis of a judgment, such as influencing the interpretation of domestic fundamental rights ('kind of effect').

Indirect effect thus has an unfortunate double-meaning as it refers either to the conditions of international law's validity in domestic law, which is indirect in the sense that it depends on an act of incorporation, and it refers to the kind of effect international law may have, not itself forming the basis of a judgment about legality, but having an indirect effect in the sphere of interpretation.

There is a further general drawback in speaking of the internal *effects* of international law. With or without an act of transformation, it might be that international law is valid in a domestic setting, but has no *effect* at all because a higher or later domestic rule sets it aside. Because of this peculiarity, it might be better to speak of *direct and indirect applicability*. It would not be odd that the law is applicable but ineffective because it is set aside on the basis of the rules of conflict in terms of legal hierarchy that apply in any given case.

But typically, direct applicability opens up another set of questions on the relationship between international and national law. Namely, under basically monist premises, the

[9] *Görülü*, German Federal Constitutional Court, 14 October 2004, docket number 2 BvR 1481/04.

fact that international law forms part of the valid law in the domestic setting does not mean that it is applicable without further ado. The question of direct applicability rather draws attention to the further conditions under which international law can be applied – conditions ensuing from the fact that international law is valid law in the first place. Specifically, the approach of direct applicability may consider whether international law is sufficiently precise or complete to be applied directly, as opposed to being vague and providing no operable standard, and whether it was intended to be applied directly.[10] While domestic legal orders may decide that international legal obligations are directly applicable, none would do so without attaching further qualifications and conditions. Thus international law might be valid domestically but not applicable. The inverse is, of course, never true: international law would not be applicable if it was not recognised as valid law in the first place.

Bearing these common usages and terminological difficulties in mind, we continue to speak of international law's (and ASEAN external agreements') *internal effects*. It strikes us as being the more encompassing term. In addition, non-applicable law has an effect if, for instance, it

---

[10] See D. Shelton, 'Introduction', in D. Shelton (ed.), *International Law and Domestic Legal Systems: Incorporation, Transformation, and Persuasion* (Oxford University Press, 2011) 1–22 at 12 (noting that 'the decisive criterion most commonly cited is whether or not the provision is sufficiently precise to be capable of judicial enforcement. Some courts have referred to this test as one of the 'self-sufficiency' of the provision.'); A. Nollkaemper, *National Courts and the International Rule of Law* (Oxford: Oxford University Press, 2011) 130–139.

('indirectly') impacts the process of interpretation. To return to the previous example: in Germany the ECHR is not applicable as a cause of action or as basis for a judgment. It still has internal effects because in a number of situations, it *must be* taken into consideration when applying and interpreting domestic law.

Finally, we prefer the term *internal effects* over another competitor, *reception*. The reason is that we want to capture both sides of the question of internal effects (domestic and international). Reception would specifically focus on the process in which international law gains validity in domestic law.[11] However, in moving beyond the domestic perspective on international law, international law itself has also something to say about its internal effects. International institutions, in particular, international courts, can and do pronounce on whether an international provision is sufficiently precise to be directly applied domestically. Against the background of these terminological clarifications, we can now better approach the internal effects of ASEAN external agreements as a product of both international law and domestic law.

5.2 Views from general international law

It is appropriate to start from the basic international law credo that it falls generally within the prerogative of states and their legal order to decide how to implement international law domestically. Domestic constitutional orders

---

[11] H. Keller, *Rezeption des Völkerrechts* (Berlin: Springer, 2003) 42.

take a stance on the internal status and effects of international law.[12] There is no further general international legal obligation that requires states to give international law a specific effect. To be clear, states incur international legal responsibility where they fail to live up to their international commitments and when they breach their international legal obligations. Such breaches then possibly trigger specific dispute settlement mechanisms or the generally applicable law of state responsibility. That is a matter of international law. In principle, the prospect of international responsibility does not change the internal effect of international law.

What is more, international law does not generally consider the existence of domestic laws, which do not conform to international obligations, to *eo ipso* amount to an international breach. The principle of good faith might suggest otherwise, namely that the mere existence of nonconforming domestic law constitutes a breach of international law.[13] Article 26 of the Vienna Convention on the Law of Treaties (VCLT) stipulates the principle of 'pacta sunt servanda'; that is, agreements must be kept. It states 'every treaty in force is binding upon the parties to it and must be

---

[12] See also S. D. Murphy, 'Does International Law Obligate States to Open Their National Courts to Persons for the Invocation of Treaty Norms That Protect or Benefit Persons?' in D. Sloss (ed.), *The Role of Domestic Courts in Treaty Enforcement: A Comparative Study* (Cambridge: Cambridge University Press, 2009) 61–119 at 70, quoting A. Cassese, *International Law* (2005) 218 (subject to some exceptions, international law generally 'leaves each country complete freedom with regard to how it fulfils, nationally, its international obligations').

[13] Murphy, 'Does International Law Obligate States' at 67.

performed by them in good faith.' The ICJ reads this principle of good faith to impose an obligation on any party to apply a treaty 'in a reasonable way and in such a manner that its purpose can be realized'.[14] But the Court does not suggest that the obligation of Article 26 VCLT is thick or strong enough to compel a specific mode of implementation or effect of international law. To be sure, the VCLT further provides that domestic law cannot justify a breach of international law (Article 27). However, this itself supports the view that the mode of implementation remains a state prerogative. If bringing national law into conformity with international law was itself already an international legal obligation, Article 27 would be superfluous.

The Permanent Court of International Justice already found in its 1925 Advisory Opinion on the *Exchange of Greek and Turkish Populations* that there exists 'a principle which is self-evident, according to which a State which has contracted valid international obligations is bound to make in its legislation such modifications as may be necessary to ensure the fulfillment of the obligations undertaken'.[15] This statement might seem to support the view that non-conforming domestic law amounts to a breach of international law. This possibly harbors the potential for a bolder claim about the internal effect of international law from the standpoint of international law. However, this was not the path this advisory

---

[14] *Gabčíkovo-Nagymaros Project (Hungary/Slovakia)*, Judgment of 25 September 1997, (1997) ICJ Reports 7, 79.

[15] *Exchange of Greek and Turkish Populations*, Advisory Opinion, PCIJ Series B no 10, 21 February 1925, para 51.

opinion or international legal doctrine has taken. Notably, the ICJ has only referred to this statement once when, in 2009, it handed down a decision in a series of cases relating to the internal effects of individual rights enshrined in the Vienna Convention on Consular Relations (VCCR)[16]. On that single occasion, the ICJ notably toned down the PCIJ's statement of 1925 and read it as just another authority in support of the uncontested proposition that domestic law cannot justify a breach of international legal obligations.[17] Other international agreements might, however, go further into such a direction. We will return to examples of specific agreements after continuing the general view from international law on direct effect.

The main basis for supporting the view that general international law claims direct effect dates far back to the Permanent Court of International Justice (PCIJ), to a decision rendered three years after the 1925 Advisory Opinion on the *Exchange of Greek and Turkish Populations*. That 1928 decision concerned the internal effects of a treaty between Poland and the free city of Danzig, the so-called *Beamtenabkommen*, which obliged Poland to accord certain working conditions to Danzig railway officials.[18] When Poland failed to do so, Danzig railway officials, who had passed into the Polish service, sued Poland in Danzig courts. Danzig first requested

[16] Vienna Convention on Consular Relations, Vienna, 24 April 1963.
[17] *Request for Interpretation of the Judgment of 31 March 2004 in the Case Concerning Avena and Other Mexican Nationals (Mexico v United States)*, Judgment of 19 January 2009, para 8.
[18] *Jurisdiction of the Courts of Danzig*, Advisory Opinion, PCIJ Series B no 15, 3 March 1928.

that the League of Nations High Commissioner for Danzig
offer a decision on whether these railway employees were
entitled to bring claims before Danzig courts based on the
Danzig-Polish treaty and whether the Polish Railways
Administration was bound to accept the jurisdiction of these
courts. The High Commissioner declined and so Danzig
persuaded the League of Nations Council to request an advisory opinion from the PCIJ on the matter.[19]

Poland maintained before the PCIJ that the *Beamtenabkommen* only created rights and obligations between the
contracting parties and, 'failing its incorporation into Polish
national legislation, [it] cannot create direct rights or obligations for the individuals concerned'.[20] Poland would only be
responsible to the free city of Danzig as it argued that the
treaty as a matter of *inter*-national law dealt only with the
relationship between Poland and Danzig and did not give
rights to individuals or create obligations for Poland *in relation to* individuals. Its responsibility, if any, was owed to
Danzig.[21]

Danzig, conversely, submitted that, in spite of the
agreement having taken the form of an international treaty,
it was 'intended by the contracting Parties to constitute part
of the 'series of provisions which establish the legal relationship between the Railways Administration and its employees'
("contract of service").[22] The court placed emphasis on the
intention of the parties and sided with Danzig. It first reiter-
ated the common credo that 'according to a well-established
principle of international law, the *Beamtenabkommen*, being

[19] *Ibid.*   [20] *Ibid.* para 35.   [21] *Ibid.* para 35.   [22] *Ibid.* para 36.

83

an international agreement, cannot, as such, create direct rights and obligations for private individuals.'[23] This was an overly broad and too categorical statement already in 1928 and, indeed, the court immediately continued that, at the same time:

> it cannot be disputed that the very object of an international agreement, according to the intention of the contracting Parties, may be the adoption by the Parties of some definite rules creating individual rights and obligations and enforceable by the national courts.[24]

It could thus be that contracting parties to international agreements decidedly aspire to create and ensure certain internal effects so that individual rights contained within an international agreement are made effective through enforcement action in domestic courts.

How may such an intention be established? Trying to plough an objective path, the PCIJ continued to locate this intention with reference to the terms of the agreement. It further supported its findings with reference to past practices in the application of the treaty:

> The fact that the various provisions were put in the form of an *Abkommen* is corroborative, but not conclusive evidence as to the character and legal effects of the instrument. The intention of the Parties, which is to be ascertained from the contents of the Agreement, taking into consideration the manner in which the Agreement has been applied, is decisive.[25]

[23] *Ibid.* para 37.   [24] *Ibid.* para 37.   [25] *Ibid.* para 37.

In conclusion:

> [t]he wording and general tenor of the *Beamtenabkommen*
> show that its provisions are directly applicable as between
> the officials and the Administration. ... According to its
> contents, the object of the *Beamtenabkommen* is to create a
> special legal régime governing the relations between the
> Polish Railways Administration and the Danzig officials,
> workmen and employees who have passed into the
> permanent service of the Polish Administration.[26]

This is the closest that international law has ever come to
demanding a specific internal effect. In fact, even here the
Court avoided doing exactly that. The Court was asked
whether an international agreement could serve as a legal
basis for claims brought by individuals before domestic
courts – whether domestic legislation *allowing* domestic
courts to apply the international treaty was in conformity
with that treaty. It was not asking, and did not pronounce
on that issue, whether Danzig was *required* to provide such a
venue and remedy.

More recently, the ICJ was again faced with the
question of internal effects in two equally famous cases concerning the application of the Vienna Convention on Consular Relations (VCCR). In both the *LaGrand*[27] and the *Avena*[28]
case, the claimants, Germany and Mexico respectively, alleged

---

[26] *Ibid.* para 38.
[27] *LaGrand (Germany v United States)*, Judgment of 27 June 2001, (2001)
ICJ Rep 466.
[28] *Avena and Other Mexican Nationals (Mexico v United States of
America)*, Judgment of 31 March 2004, (2004) ICJ Rep 12.

that the United States had violated the VCCR by not informing the arrested foreign nationals of their rights under the convention.[29] Other claims pertained to issues of state responsibility for domestic legislation and for domestic judgments and, critically, to the question of whether the United States had breached its treaty obligations by not allowing judicial review of the death sentences issued against the accused in order to remedy possible violations of the Vienna Convention and to render its provisions effective.[30] The question here was precisely whether the VCCR *required* the United States and other state parties to give that treaty certain internal effects (i.e. judicial review on the domestic level if the VCCR was allegedly breached).

The treaty does not explicitly provide for its internal effect. It states in the relevant Article 36(2) 2 that:

> The rights referred to in paragraph 1 of this article shall be exercised in conformity with the laws and regulations of the receiving State, subject to the proviso, however, that the said laws and regulations must *enable full effect to be given to the purposes for which the rights accorded under this article are intended.*

The rights spelled out in paragraph 1 include, for instance, the freedom of foreign nationals to communicate and have access to their consular officers. Paragraph 1 also provides that the arrested person of foreign nationality shall be informed 'of his

[29] Art. 36(1)(a) and (c) VCCR.
[30] *LaGrand (Germany v United States)*, Judgment of 27 June 2001, (2001) ICJ Rep 466.

rights under this subparagraph'[31]. The Unites States argued that the Vienna Convention neither establishes individual rights, nor does it obliges parties to remedy possible breaches of the convention through their criminal justice system. The court sided with the applicant, Germany, and found that the convention did create individual rights. It stressed the fact that Article 26(1) of the VCCR speaks of 'his rights'. In the opinion of the court, the clarity of this provision 'admits of no doubt'.[32] But even if there are individual rights, that fact alone does not settle the question of whether not allowing judicial review amounted to a breach. What does international law, in the form of VCCR obligations, require on the domestic level?

The issue of direct effect and requisite remedies was a more difficult one. It is not clear what is required by the provision stating that 'laws and regulations must enable full effect to be given to the purposes for which the rights accorded under this article are intended'. Part of that question of what is meant by that relates to the so-called procedural default rule of US law, which provides that a defendant in criminal proceedings can only raise a new issue before a federal court in *habeas corpus* proceedings by showing cause (having been prevented from raising the claim earlier) and prejudice.[33] Does such a procedural default rule violate the VCCR? Not as such, the court found, but the way in which the rule was applied in the concrete case effectively prevented

[31] Art. 36, para 1, lit. b. VCCR.
[32] *LaGrand (Germany v United States)*, Judgment of 27 June 2001, (2001) ICJ Rep 466, para 77.
[33] *Ibid.* para 23.

the defendants from challenging their conviction and thus violated Article 36(2).[34] The application of the default rule prevented the giving of 'full effect' to convention rights.[35]

The judgment, together with its very similar reiteration in *Avena*, has sometimes been read to oblige the United States to provide an individual with meaningful access to U.S. courts to vindicate his or her rights under the VCLT.[36] But such a reading does not seem warranted. The court did, in fact, order that the United States 'shall allow the review and reconsideration of the conviction and sentence by taking account of the violation of the rights set forth in that Convention.'[37] But it shall (and can) do so, according to the court, 'by means of its own choosing'.[38] Allowing for direct effect and applicability would certainly be a straightforward remedy, but other remedies are equally conceivable.[39] Thus, the court did not require the US to grant individuals access to judicial (review) proceedings in order to give full effect to the individual rights enshrined in the VCCR.[40]

In sum, as a matter of general international law and jurisprudence the general credo remains that it falls within the

---

[34] *Ibid.* para 91.
[35] See P.-M. Dupuy and C. Hoss, 'LaGrand Case (Germany v United States of America)', in R. Wolfrum (ed.), *Max Planck Encyclopedia of Public International Law* (Oxford: Oxford University Press, 2009) para 19;
[36] Murphy, 'Does International Law Obligate States' at 61.
[37] *LaGrand (Germany v United States)*, Judgment of 27 June 2001, (2001) ICJ Rep 466, para 128.
[38] *Ibid.*   [39] See Dupuy and Hoss, 'LaGrand Case', para 43.
[40] See further, Nollkaemper, *National Courts and the International Rule of Law* at 119.

prerogative of states and their legal order to decide how to implement international law domestically. More specifically, even when an international agreement explicitly or, leaning on intentions, implicitly creates rights for individuals, that does not mean that states are obliged to give effect to those rights, for instance, by granting individual rights holders access to judicial procedures to vindicate their rights. How individual rights are to be given effect again largely falls within the prerogative of states.

One might think that this reading of state preroga-tives gives rise to an obligation of result, rather than an obligation of specific conduct. Such a distinction between obligations of means (or conduct), on the one hand, and obli-gations of result, on the other, is not uncommon.[41] But the distinction has given rise to some intricate difficulties and the ILC Draft Articles on State Responsibility are conspicu-ously silent on this distinction.[42] At first glance, it might seem straightforward in a number of constellations. An obligation of result sets a certain target and leaves the choice of means to the states. A typical example would be the Kyoto Protocol on Climate Change, which requires states to adhere to a certain maximum quota of carbon emissions. How they reach that quota is left to them. Conversely, one could think of a treaty prescribing a specific conduct, such as of the type contained

[41] C. P. Economides, 'Content of the Obligation: Obligations of Means and Obligations of Result', in J. Crawford, A. Pellet and S. Olleson (eds.), *The Law of International Responsibility* (Oxford University Press, 2010) 371–381; Murphy, 'Does International Law Obligate States' at 74.
[42] Economides, 'Content of the Obligation' at 376–377.

in many economic agreements when they prohibit quantitative trade restrictions. Any conduct amounting to a quantitative trade restriction amounts to a breach, period. There is little leeway, if any. But as the cases centered on the VCCR show, seemingly specific rights and obligations often times allow for different ways of conduct.

When it comes to the kind of obligation and the link to internal effects, obligations of result hardly compel specific internal action. An example may be taken from the *Agreement Establishing the ASEAN-Australia-New Zealand Free Trade Area*, whose Customs Procedures provide that '[t]he customs administrations of the parties will encourage consultation with each other regarding significant customs issues that affect goods traded among the parties.'[43] Conversely, obligations of means or conduct demand and not only 'encourage' specific action. They might be very explicit in what they require domestically and might even explicitly demand direct applicability. This is often the case for human rights instruments providing, such as CEDAW, that parties 'ensure through competent national tribunals and other public institutions the effective protection of women against any act of discrimination'.[44] This brings us to the discussion of specific requirements regarding the internal effects, not of international law generally, but of specific international legal provisions. It is from this combination of general and specific

---

[43] Art. 12 Customs Procedures, Agreement Establishing the ASEAN-Australia-New Zealand Free Trade Area.
[44] Art. 2(c) CEDAW.

law that we can distil the general framework also for assessing the internal effects of ASEAN external agreements.

5.3 Requirements of specific legal instruments and regimes

While international law generally does not require any specific effects of international law in domestic legal orders, particular treaty provisions might provide for specific effects such as direct applicability and access to courts. Not conforming to such obligations to grant the treaty such specific effects would then amount to a treaty violation.

In his detailed study of the question 'Does International Law Obligate States to Open Their National Courts to Persons for the Invocation of Treaty Norms That Protect or Benefit Persons?', Sean Murphy points out that for a while, treaties of friendship, commerce and navigation typically allowed persons and corporations access to local courts.[45] That may be correct but misses the point in two respects: first, the question is not whether states may allow foreign nationals access to their courts, but whether international law obliges them to do so; second, having access to courts itself says nothing about the applicability of international law. Even if a treaty provided that nationals of one contracting party shall have unhindered access to the domestic justice system, an important point in itself, it is an altogether different question which rights they may actually be able to vindicate in this way.

---

[45] Murphy, 'Does International Law Obligate States' at 88.

Bilateral Investment Treaties (BITs) – which are in some ways a modern continuation of the treaties of friendship – do not usually oblige the contracting parties to open their domestic courts to foreign investors to vindicate their rights under domestic or international law. While they typically provide standards of protection such as prohibitions against the denial of justice and of fair and equitable treatment, which may bear on issues of court access, they also oblige contracting parties to accept the jurisdiction of one or more fora of international arbitration. Where a provision on the internal effects *can*, however, be found is at the stage of the enforcement of arbitral awards. BITs tend to oblige parties to enforce arbitral awards as 'final and absolute ruling under domestic law'.[46] The Convention on the Settlement of Investment Disputes between States and Nationals of Other States[47] (ICSID Convention) also provides that awards rendered within the framework of the International Center for the Settlement of Investment Disputes (ICSID) shall be recognised by each contracting party as binding, 'as if it were a final judgment of a court in that State'.[48] Parties seeking recognition or enforcement of an arbitral award can, according to the

---

[46] German Model BIT of 2012, Art. 10(3).

[47] Washington, 18 March 1965, entered into force 14 October 1966.

[48] Art. 54(1) ICSID Convention. See in further detail S. Choi, 'Judicial Enforcement of Arbitration Awards under the ICSID and New York Conventions' (1995–1996) 28 *NYU Journal of International Law & Politics* 175–216; S. A. Alexandrov, 'Enforcement of ICSID Awards: Articles 53 and 54 of the ICSID Convention', in C. Binder et al. (eds.), *International Investment Law for the 21st Century. Essays in Honour of Christoph Schreuer* (Oxford: Oxford University Press, 2009).

Convention, turn to the competent court or other authority of any contracting state.[49] Contracting states are thus obliged to give effect to the international arbitral awards in their domestic systems.

Such provisions specifically demand that domestic legislation be adopted to allow for contracting parties to actually meet their international obligations. Non-conformity of legislation can then amount to a breach of international law without further implementing or executing action. The London Convention on the Prevention of Marine Pollution by Dumping of Wastes and Other Matter is another case in point. It provides that all contracting parties 'shall prohibit the dumping of any wastes'.[50] Other international instruments explicitly contain an obligation to legislate; the Convention on the Prevention and Punishment of the Crime of Genocide[51] and the International Convention on the Elimination of all Forms of Racial Discrimination serve as examples in this regard.[52]

What is of especial note in going further in its demand for internal effects is the specific context of international trade law. The well-known clause Article XVI:4 of the WTO Agreement establishes that '[e]ach Member shall ensure the conformity of its laws, regulations and administrative procedures with its obligations as provided in the

---

[49] Art. 54(2) ICSID Convention.
[50] London Convention on the Prevention of Marine Pollution by Dumping of Wastes and Other Matter 1972, Art. 4(1)
[51] Adopted 9 December 1948, entered into force 12 January 1951, 78 UNTS 277.
[52] Opened for signature 7 March 1966, entered into force 4 January 1969, 660 UNTS 195.

annexed Agreements.' Non-conformity of domestic laws, regulations, and administrative procedures can thus by itself amount to a breach of international law. No further executing act of any kind is required for there to be a breach. The existence of non-conforming law is sufficient.[53] As the Panel elaborated in *EC – IT Products*, Article XVI:4 WTO Agreement means that 'a Member is obliged to ensure that its domestic legislation is consistent'.[54] In *US – Section Trade Act*, the Panel found that the General Agreement on Tariffs and Trade (GATT), now confirmed by Article XVI:4 WTO Agreement 'make abundantly clear that legislation as such, independently from its application in specific cases, may breach GATT/WTO obligations'.[55] But Article XVI:4 does not require specific internal effects of (international) WTO law in domestic legal orders. The provision still falls short of demanding a specific domestic status or effect of international law. WTO jurisprudence has not taken the article into that direction either. The consequence of domestic laws, regulations, and administrative procedures falling short of WTO norms would constitute a breach of international law. Article XVI:4 does not require states to give individuals access to their courts and to allow them to invoke international legal obligations to possibly challenge inconsistent domestic laws.

[53] Panel Report, *US – Section 301 Trade Act*, WT/DS152/R, 22 December 1999, paras 7.41–7.42.

[54] Panel Report, *EC – IT Products*, WT/DS375/R, 16 August 2010, fn. 42.

[55] Panel Report, *US – Section 301 Trade Act*, WT/DS 152/R, 22 December 1999, paras 7.41. See also Panel Report, *EC – IT Products*, WT/DS375/R, 16 August 2010, fn 42 ('a Member is obliged to ensure that its domestic legislation is consistent with the concessions contained in its Schedule.').

Next to international investment law, the legal regime that, goes furthest in its demands of internal effects is that of human rights, especially in its regional manifestations. Article 13 of the ECHR contains the 'right to an effective remedy' and provides that '[e]veryone whose rights and freedoms as set forth in this Convention are violated shall have an effective remedy before a national authority.' The ECtHR has itself suggested that giving direct effect to the ECHR would further strengthen the system, encourage domestic courts to take a more proactive stance, and advised that Member States allow for direct applicability.[56] But the ECtHR stops short of *demanding* that the Convention have direct effect. In *Kudla v Poland* it held that:

> Article 13, giving *direct expression* [not direct effect, LT/IV] to the States' obligation to protect human rights first and foremost within their own legal system, establishes an additional guarantee for an individual in order to ensure that he or she effectively enjoys those rights.[57]

The ECtHR is certainly most adamant that the rights enshrined in the Convention be made effective. In a stream of decisions, it has fleshed out a principle of effectiveness in applying the Convention, elaborating that '[t]he Convention is intended to guarantee not rights that are theoretical or

---

[56] A. Stone Sweet and H. Keller, *A Europe of Rights: The Impact of the ECHR on National Legal Systems* (Oxford: Oxford University Press, 2008) 708.

[57] *Kudla v Poland* (appl. no. 30210/96), Judgment (Grand Chamber), 26 October 2000, Reports 2000-XI, 197, para 152, cited in Stone Sweet and Keller, *A Europe of Rights,* at 708.

illusory but rights that are practical and effective'.[58] In spite of this trajectory, the ways in which Member States meet these demands are of their own choosing. The ECtHR does not require that the Convention be directly applicable before domestic courts. That is not to say that the domestic laws of many Member States do not treat the Convention as directly applicable. Some members even grant it supra-constitutional status.[59]

The picture is notably different when it comes to the Inter-American Convention on Human Rights (IACHR). The Inter-American Court embraced a monist approach and required that the IACHR and its judgments be given direct effect.[60] The IACHR further held that domestic courts are prohibited from applying domestic law contrary to the convention. Instead they should directly apply the Convention and test domestic law against it in a form of 'decentralized conventionality control (*control de convencionalidad*)'.[61]

Global instruments, such as the International Covenant on Civil and Political Rights (ICCPR) contain wording similar to that of Article 13 ECHR (providing for an effective remedy). However, similar to the ECHR, such an article has not been interpreted so as to demand that the ICCPR be

---

[58] ECtHR, *Airey v Ireland*, Judgment of 9 October 1979, Series A No. 41, para 26; *Artico v Italy*, Judgment of 13 May 1980 Series A No. 37, para 33.
[59] In detail, see Stone Sweet and Keller, *A Europe of Rights*.
[60] C. Binder, 'The Prohibition of Amnesties by the Inter-American Court of Human Rights', in A. von Bogdandy and I. Venzke (eds.), *International Judicial Lawmaking: On Public Authority and Democratic Legitimation in Global Governance* (Berlin: Springer, 2012) 279.
[61] *Ibid.*

directly applicable.[62] Again, some domestic courts treat it as such, but that is not a requirement of international treaty law. The ICCPR does however contain the softly worded obligation that 'each State Party to the present Covenant undertakes to take the necessary steps, in accordance with its constitutional processes and with the provisions of the present Covenant, to adopt such laws or other measures as may be necessary to give effect to the rights recognized in the present Covenant (Article 2(2) ICCPR).'[63]

With respect to ASEAN specifically, attention should be paid to Member States' obligations under the strongly worded and rather broad Article 5 ASEAN Charter. It provides that 'Member States shall take all necessary measures, including the enactment of appropriate domestic legislation, to effectively implement the provisions of this Charter and to comply with all obligations of membership.' This indicates that domestic legislation itself, even if not applied, or possibly the failure to enact legislation as well, could amount to a breach of the Charter.

5.4 The view from European law

One of the main differences of European law in comparison to international law rests precisely in the fact that the former claims direct effect in domestic legal systems, at least when

---

[62] D. Desierto, ASEAN ITL Project, Country Report on the Philippines.

[63] A. Seibert-Fohr 'Domestic Implementation of the International Covenant on Civil and Political Rights Pursuant to Its Article 2 para 2' (2001) 5 *Max Planck Yearbook of United Nations Law* 399–472.

the provisions of a legally binding European instrument are sufficiently clear, precise, and unconditional so that they are justiciable and can be relied upon before domestic courts.[64] Such a requirement for direct effect was first established in relation to the foundational treaty of the European Economic Community (EEC) itself and later extended to instruments of secondary legislation, as well as external agreements of the EU with third parties. The ECJ laid the cornerstone of this development with its judgment in the case of *Van Gend & Loos* in which the Dutch company of that name complained before the Dutch *Tariefkommissie* (an administrative tribunal) that the increase in import duties violated Article 12 of the EEC Treaty.[65] The *Tariefkommissie* asked the ECJ for a preliminary ruling on the question:

> whether Article 12 of the EEC Treaty has direct application within the territory of a Member State, in other words, whether nationals of such a State can, on the basis of the Article in question, lay claim to individual rights which the courts must protect[66]

---

[64] For the similarities but also notable differences between the claims of international and European law see F. Martines, 'Direct Effect of International Agreements of the European Union' (2014) 25 *European Journal of International Law* 129–147.

[65] For a recent re-assessment see D. Chalmers and L. Barroso, 'What Van Gend en Loos Stands For' (2014) 12 *International Journal of Constitutional Law* 105–134; insightfully on the making of the judgment in its aftermath A. Vauchez, 'The Transnational Politics of Judicialization. Van Gend en Loos and the Making of European Union Polity' (2010) 16 *European Law Journal* 1.

[66] Case 26/62 *Van Gend & Loos* [1963] ECR 1 at 3.

The court replied that:

> [t]he objective of the EEC Treaty, which is to establish a
> Common Market, the functioning of which is of direct
> concern to interested parties in the Community, implies
> that this Treaty is more than an agreement, which merely
> creates mutual obligations between the contracting states.
> This view is confirmed by the preamble to the Treaty,
> which refers not only to governments but also to peoples.
> It is also confirmed more specifically by the establishment
> of institutions endowed with sovereign rights, the exercise
> of which affects Member States and their citizens.
>
> . . .
>
> Community constitutes a new legal order of international
> law for the benefit of which the states have limited their
> sovereign rights . . . and the subjects of which comprise not
> only Member States but also their nationals.[67]

Against this background, it further held that 'Article 12 contains
a clear and unconditional prohibition'[68] that is not qualified by
any reservation or whose implementation is conditional on
further legislative measures. The answer was thus yes, 'Article
12 must be interpreted as producing direct effects and creating
individual rights which national courts must protect.'[69] Moreover, the court opined that the invocability of European law in
domestic proceedings further adds to the supervision and
enforcement of European law, in addition to the roles that the
European Commission and other Member States play in this
regard. The key rationale for the Court to give direct effect to

---

[67] *Ibid.* at 12.   [68] *Ibid.* at 13.   [69] *Ibid.* at 13.

provisions of the EEC Treaty thus stemmed from the nature and aims of the Community as well as from the belief that its existence and ambition would be hampered, if not undermined, if the treaty had no direct effect.

The conditions of direct effect of European law have evolved significantly ever since.[70] By and large the thresholds have decreased, and the doctrine has been projected beyond the provisions of the EEC Treaty to the secondary acts of regulations, decisions, directives and also, to external agreements. Out of the numerous intricate issues pertaining to the conditions under which European law claims each of these instruments to be directly effective in the legal orders of the Member States, it should first be highlighted that the effect of directives is particularly complicated as they, in principle, impose obligations of certain results and leave discretion to Member States in the implementation process with regard to how to achieve those results.[71] It is in this context that the ECJ has developed the notion of indirect effect in combination with the principle of harmonious interpretation.

Again subject to further conditions, a directive can only have direct effect in vertical relations where a case is

---

[70] From the rich literature on the issue, see P. Pescatore, 'The Doctrine of "Direct Effect": An Infant Disease of Community Law' (1983) 8 *European Law Review* 155; S. Prechal, 'Direct Effect, Indirect Effect, Supremacy and the Evolving Constitution of the European Union', in C. Barnard (ed.), *The Fundamentals of EU Law Revisited: Assessing the Impact of the Constitutional Debate* (Oxford: Oxford University Press, 2007) 35–69.

[71] See generally S. Prechal, *Directives in EC Law*, 2nd edn. (Oxford: Oxford University Press, 2005).

brought against a public body and not at all in horizontal relations where a case is brought against an individual.[72] But even in a vertical dimension where a directive does not have direct effect because it is not justiciable for one reason or another (because it is insufficiently clear, precise or conditional on further legislative measures), it can all the same have *indirect* effect that works on the level of interpretation. At its core, the notion of indirect effect, in combination with the principle of harmonious interpretation, demands that national law be interpreted *in the light of* directives.[73]

The courts' jurisprudence has nurtured the principle of harmonious interpretation over time, specifically with reference to Member States' obligation expressed in ex-Article 10 EC Treaty 'to take all appropriate measures ... to ensure fulfillment of the obligations arising out of this Treaty or resulting from action taken by the institutions of the Community'. This wording and the court's stance on this issue have now informed Article 4(3) TEU articulating the principle of sincere cooperation:

Article 4(3) TEU

Pursuant to the principle of sincere cooperation, the Union and the Member States shall, in full mutual respect, assist each other in carrying out tasks which flow from the Treaties.

---

[72] Case 152/84, *Marshall v Southampton and South-West Hampshire Area Health Authority* [1986] ECR 723 para 48.

[73] Case 14/83, *Von Colson and Kamann v Land Nordrhein-Westfalen* [1984] ECR 189 para 26-8.

> The Member States shall take any appropriate measure, general or particular, to ensure fulfillment of the obligations arising out of the Treaties or resulting from the acts of the institutions of the Union.

> The Member States shall facilitate the achievement of the Union's tasks and refrain from any measure which could jeopardise the attainment of the Union's objectives.

With a view to sincere co-operation and aiming at the full effectiveness of European law, national courts and other domestic authorities are required to interpret national law in the light of European law. Such an obligation not only exists in a vertical dimension where directives are used in cases brought against public bodies, but also in a horizontal dimension, where *direct* effect is so far ruled out.[74] The principle of harmonious interpretation has furthermore repeatedly been qualified as a strong interpretative obligation that does not require *contra legem* claims, but it does shift the factors influencing interpretation when compared to inter-pretations under national law alone.[75]

In sum, in contrast to international law, EU law generally requires that Member States give direct effect to European law. Even where the conditions for direct effect

---

[74] Case C-106/89 *Marleasing SA v La Comercial Internacionale de Alimentacion SA* [1990] ECR I–4135.

[75] See M. W. Hesselink, 'A Toolbox for European Judges' (2011) 17 *European Law Journal* 441–469, at 448; P. Craig, 'The Legal Effect of Directives: Policy, Rules and Exceptions' (2009) 34 *European Law Review* 349–377, at 362.

are not met, it relies on principles of sincere co-operation and harmonious interpretation to require that European law be taken into account in the application of domestic law. On this level of harmonious interpretation there is again some overlap with general international law, which is frequently also effective domestically, owing to demands of consistent interpretation.[76]

5.5 The view from domestic law

Above all, the effect that international law might have depends on the choices made by the domestic legal order. That does not, however, render international law silent with regard to the effects that it has domestically. Rather, whatever the choice of domestic law may be in principle, the internal effects of international law also depend on a number of features and criteria of the international legal provisions at issue. For instance, is it sufficiently precise to be directly applicable before domestic courts?

As mentioned briefly above, it is common to group domestic legal orders within categories of monist and dualist

---

[76] G. Betlem and A. Nollkaemper, 'Giving Effect to Public International Law and European Community Law before Domestic Courts. A Comparative Analysis of the Practice of Consistent Interpretation' (2003) 14 *European Journal of International Law* 569–589; A. Alì, 'Some Reflections on the Principle of Consistent Interpretation through the Case Law of the European Court of Justice', in N. Boschiero et al. (eds.), *International Courts and the Development of International Law. Essays in Honour of Tullio Treves* (Berlin: Springer, 2013) 881–895.

systems when it comes to the question of which status or effect they generally give to international law.[77] Even if it is understood that these categories are porous and better treated as ideal types located on a spectrum of possibilities, their heuristic value is ultimately questionable because many domestic legal orders mix elements of both. Since these notions continue to shape the constitutional legal discourse within ASEAN Member States and beyond, we continue to employ them with these caveats attached.

Overall, the kind of international law that is at issue tends to be more determinative of its internal effects than the monist or dualist outlook of the domestic legal.[78] Conversely, even if the effect of international law depends above all on the choice of domestic legal orders, domestic legal orders tend to converge on how they treat certain kinds of international law. For example, a number of constitutional orders grant human rights treaties direct effect and a status superior to parliamentary legislation but they would not do

---

[77] For a historical overview of debates with that vocabulary see Finegan, 'Neither Dualism nor Monism'; further see G. Gaja, 'Dualism: A Review', in J. Nijman and A. Nollkaemper (eds.), *New Perspectives on the Divide between National and International Law* (Oxford University Press, 2007) 52–62.

[78] A. Aust, *Modern Treaty Law and Practice* (Cambridge: Cambridge University Press, 2007) 182; A. Nollkaemper and J. E. Nijman, 'Beyond the Divide', in A. Nollkaemper and J. E. Nijman (eds.), *New Perspectives on the Divide Between National and International Law* (Oxford: Oxford University Press, 2007) 341–360 (notably arguing that soft law instruments can enter domestic legal orders more easily, contributing to the perforation of borders between legal orders).

so for a treaty setting fishing quotas.[79] To describe a legal order as either monist or dualist often times does not improve our understanding because so much depends on what kind of international law is at issue.[80] The categories may still help in outlining the possible choices that domestic legal orders can make with regard to the internal effects of international law.

Two main choices are fundamental. First, does international law potentially have direct effect? In other words, before it becomes operative in the domestic legal order, does it require an act of incorporation or not? Second, with or without an act of incorporation, what is the effect of international law? This includes questions on international laws' rank and on its more general relationship with other law. These two main choices about incorporation and rank of international law set up a rough matrix of four possibilities (see Table 5.1 below):

5.5.1 Dualism

In his influential early account on the relationship between international and municipal law, Heinrich Triepel found,

[79] Cf. the overview in Shelton, 'Introduction' at 1 ('There also appears to be a trend to give human rights treaties preferential treatment in domestic constitutions.'); Nollkaemper and Nijman 'Beyond the Divide' (pointing to common values as an explanatory factor in this regard).

[80] A. von Bogdandy, 'Pluralism, Direct Effect, and the Ultimate Say: On the Relationship Between International and Domestic Constitutional Law' (2008) 6 *International Journal of Constitutional Law* 397–413.

Table 5.1

| | | Incorporation of international law: direct effect? | |
		Yes / 'Monist'	No / 'Dualist'
Rank of international law?	'High'	A: international law directly effective, trumping earlier and later domestic legal acts	C: international law only effective upon incorporation, then trumping earlier and later domestic legal acts
	'Low'	B: international law directly effective, but possibly set aside by later domestic legal acts	D: international law only effective upon incorporation, then possibly set aside by later domestic legal acts

first of all, that the two spheres of law dealt with categorically different matters. They differed, above all, in what they took to be the subjects of the law. On Triepel's reading at the time, international law was concerned with inter-state relations and only knew states as its subjects. This was obviously quite different from municipal law.[81] Not the least due to the structural transformation of international law itself – expanding in terms of subject matter and recognising individuals as subjects of the law – a distinction between international and municipal law can no longer be maintained on that basis.[82]

---

[81] H. Triepel, *Völkerrecht und Landesrecht* (Leipzig: Hirschfeldt, 1899).

[82] See on those transformations the classic work of W. G. Friedmann, *The Changing Structure of International Law* (New York, NY: Columbia University Press, 1964). Also see A. Peters, *Jenseits der Menschenrechte:*

If the nature of legal subjects and the subject matter no longer qualify as baselines for distinguishing municipal from international law in a dualist account, today the emphasis rests on the role of the legislator in incorporating international law into the domestic legal order. In dualist accounts, international law is only applicable when it is *transformed* into domestic law (the way in which it is transformed is also significant). In domestic settings before domestic courts, it would then, strictly speaking, not be international law that is applied, but domestic law incorporating and transforming international law (models C and D in the matrix above). The case of Singapore offers a rather straightforward example 'unless legislation has been specifically enacted and in force to give effect to the rights and obligations created by international agreements, even where ratified by Singapore, they have no direct effect under domestic law.'[83] That is also the typical situation in other ASEAN Member States.[84] In Malaysia, domestic law generally prevails in cases of conflict with international law.[85] One court case held specifically that

Die Rechtsstellung des Individuums im Völkerrecht (Tübingen: Mohr Siebeck, 2014).

[83] E. Tan, ASEAN ITL Project, Country Report on Singapore at 10.

[84] A. Alias and S. Lutchman, ASEAN ITL Project, Country Report on Malaysia at 21–2; Country Report on Thailand at 37.

[85] In *Kok Wah Kuan v Pengarah Penjara Kajang, Selangor Darul Ehsan* ((2004) 5 Malayan Law Journal 193 at 224) the High Court said it could not apply Article 40 (fair trial) of the Convention on the Rights of the Child (Malaysia had acceded to it) as it remained unincorporated and therefore in the realm of the Executive. It would be considered a matter of 'judicial vandalism or judicial trespass' rather than interpretation, for the High Court to apply a provision from an unincorporated treaty. See

'the Courts here must take the law as they find it expressed in the Enactments. It is not the duty of a Judge or a Magistrate to consider whether the law so set forth is contrary to international law or not.'[86]

It is the act of transformation that typically determines the rank of international law in the municipal order. In dualist settings, the act of transformation itself amounts to the source of domestic legal obligations and its rank then depends on the respective normative hierarchy enshrined in domestic constitutions or developed in legal practice. If international law is enacted as a statute, it typically has the same rank as any other statute.[87] That also means that, within the domestic context, later statutes might also set it aside. The way Singapore treats international law again serves as an example: the *lex posterior* rule is applicable to domestic statues. It is immaterial in that regard whether any of them incorporate international law.[88] A statute incorporating a treaty supersedes prior domestic law of the same or lower rank, but later

Alias and Lutchman, ASEAN ITL Project; A. Ghafur Hamdi and K. Maung Sein, 'Judicial Application of International Law in Malaysia' (2005) 1 *Asia Pacific Yearbook of International Law* 196–214, at 198.

[86] *Public Prosecutor v Wah Ah Jee*, F.M.S. Supreme Court, (1919), 2 F.M.S.L.R. 193).

[87] P.-M. Dupuy, 'International Law and Domestic (Municipal) Law', in R. Wolfrum (ed.), *Max Planck Encyclopedia of Public International Law* (Oxford: Oxford University Press, 2012) para 55; M. P. Van Alstine, 'The Role of Domestic Courts in Treaty Enforcement: Summary and Conclusions', in D. Sloss (ed.), *The Role of Domestic Courts in Treaty Enforcement: A Comparative Study* (Cambridge: Cambridge University Press, 2009) 555–613 at 577.

[88] E. Tan, Country Report on Singapore at 11, 24.

statutory legislation could then again set aside the 'internal effect' of the international treaty. Outside the context of ASEAN, the legal order of the United Kingdom is exemplary in this regard. As Anthony Aust summarizes 'the provisions of a treaty that are made part of (incorporated into) domestic law have the status only of domestic law, and can be amended or repealed by later legislation.'[89] (This corresponds to model D.) Such amendment or repeal can even be done by legislation, or by executive action.

In fact, in states that may broadly be considered dualist, the legislature may and does delegate power to the executive to transform international obligations.[90] So it is not necessarily the legislature itself that transforms and incorporates. Other state organs may do so as well. All countries have a series of different modes of implementation that arrange the division of powers between the parliament and the executive.[91]

Domestic statues may further demand that specific treaties, or international law generally, be respected, even if it has not been incorporated. An example stems from the Australian High Court when it was faced with a petition in which the claimants argued that the Australian Broadcasting Authority (ABA) had enacted regulations that were contrary

[89] A. Aust, 'United Kingdom', in D. Sloss (ed.), *The Role of Domestic Courts in Treaty Enforcement: A Comparative Study* (Cambridge: Cambridge University Press, 2009) 476–503 at 478.

[90] Van Alstine, 'The Role of Domestic Courts in Treaty Enforcement', 569.

[91] K. Pinseethong, ASEAN ITL Project, Country Report on Thailand at 38; E. Tan, Country Report on Singapore at 14–15.

to a bilateral free trade agreement between Australia and New Zealand.[92] The High Court held that the ABA was precluded from acting inconsistently with the free-trade agreement even if the free-trade agreement had not been incorporated.[93] That legal effect was supported by domestic statute. But in another case, the High Court found that administrative discretion had to be exercised in a manner which conformed with, in this case, the unincorporated Convention on the Rights of the Child. The reasoning supporting this demand is noteworthy. The court argued that Australia's ratification of the treaty created 'legitimate expectation' on the part of individuals that government officials would act accordingly.[94] Thus even unincorporated international law can create internal effects in dualist states, for instance by shaping the room of maneuver of administrations.[95]

---

[92] See D. R. Rothwell, 'Australia', in D. Sloss (ed.), *The Role of Domestic Courts in Treaty Enforcement: A Comparative Study* (Cambridge: Cambridge University Press, 2009) 120–165 at 141–143.

[93] *Ibid.*   [94] *Ibid.*

[95] It should be noted, however, that the later Teoh Case criticised this approach for bringing in international law through the back door, *Teoh v Minister for Immigration* (1995) 183 CLR 273. Furthermore, later statutory legislation seems to largely forestall giving unincorporated international law such internal effects in the cases such as these, see in further detail M. Groves, 'Is Teoh's Case Still Good Law' (2007) 14 *Australian Journal of Administrative Law* 126. See also S. Roberts, 'Minister of State for Immigration and Ethnic Affairs v Ah Hin Teoh: The High Court Decision and the Government's Reaction To It' (1995) 2 *Australian Journal of Human Rights* 135: www.austlii.edu.au/au/journals/AJHR/1995/10.html#fnB31 (sets forth government statement 'reversing' Teoh).

The interpretative practice of mostly dualist states differs to the extent that it adds to the effect of international law. The interpretative methodology could, on the one hand, not take into consideration at all the fact that the 'origin' of the domestic statue is actually a treaty, and treat the incorporating statue like any other statute that has no link with international law. On the other hand, such a link might well be taken into consideration, for instance, by giving more attention to international jurisprudence when interpreting the domestic legal provision at issue. The legislature can, to some extent, signal how close it sees the ties of the incorporating statue with international law. It could, for instance, visibly sever those ties by redrafting international legal obligations in the statute, even with some amendments and additions. It could also demonstrate close ties with international law by just annexing ('scheduling') an international treaty to an incorporating statute. Both are common practice.

It is a general approach of the interpretative practice of in principle dualist states that they demand, subject to further conditions, that domestic law be interpreted in conformity with international law where there is discretion to do so. That was the position that the German *Bundesverfassungsgericht* took in its prominent *Görgülü* decision, in which it demanded that domestic fundamental guarantees be interpreted by paying due regard to the ECHR as interpreted by the ECtHR.[96] Singapore follows England and other common law countries in upholding the presumption that domestic legal instruments are consistent with treaty

---

[96] *Görülü*, BVerfG, 14 October 2004, docket number 2 BvR 1481/04.

obligations.[97] However, if a statute is clear, it must be applied even if in breach of international law. The reason for this is that 'a court operating in a parliamentary democracy is bound to implement the will of Parliament as embodied in domestic legislation, insofar as such legislation is not incompatible with the constitution'.[98]

Variations of a presumption of conformity with international law cut across legal orders and also matter in constitutional arrangements that are primarily monist. In US law a similar position is known as the *Charming Betsy* doctrine, named after *Murray v The Schooner Charming Betsy*, where the US Supreme Court held that acts of Congress should be interpreted, where at all possible, so as not to violate international law.[99] The American Law Institute's Third Restatement of Foreign Relations summarizes that wherever 'fairly possible', domestic statutes should be interpreted so as not to conflict with international law.[100] Since

---

[97] *The Sahand* [2011] 2 SLR 1093, Singaporean case following UK case: *ex p Brind* [1991] 1 AC 696. See also *Public Prosecutor v Tan Cheng Yew* and another appeal [2013] 1 SLR 1095 where the High Court stated at [56]: 'It is trite law that Singapore follows a dualist position. In short, Singapore's international law obligations do not give rise to individual rights and obligations in the domestic context unless and until transposed into domestic law by legislation ...'.

[98] Yong Vui Kong v PP [2015] SGCA 11 at [33].

[99] *Murray v The Schooner Charming Betsy*, 6 U.S. (2 Cranch) 64 (1804).

[100] American Law Institute, Third Restatement of Foreign Relations Law (1987), para 114. See von Bogdandy, 'Pluralism, Direct Effect, and the Ultimate Say', 2; C. A. Bradley, 'The *Charming Betsy* Canon and Separation of Powers: Rethinking the Interpretive Role of International Law' (1997) 86 *Georgetown Law Journal* 479–537.

this form of internal effect is pervasive, truly important, and since it works largely independently of whether a constitutional order is primarily dualist or monist, we dedicate a separate section to it below after outlining the default position of monist constitutional arrangements.

5.5.2 *Monism*

An idealised monist legal system would treat international law as directly effective in domestic contexts without an act of incorporation by the legislature or other state organs.[101] There is, in fact, only a single legal system. But there is no country in the world that would treat *all* of its international legal obligations as directly effective.

Monist systems typically draw a number of distinctions and formulate further conditions under which international law may be directly effective. They also tend to deal differently with treaty and customary international law. What treaty law is concerned, treaty provisions need to be self-executing.[102] A provision is self-executing precisely when it can be applied without further legislative action (in the

---

[101] Aust, *Modern Treaty Law and Practice*, 181–195.

[102] C. M. Vazquez, 'The Four Doctrines of Self-Executing Treaties' (1995) 89 *American Journal of International Law* 695–723; T. Buergenthal, 'Self-Executing and Non-Self-Executing Treaties in National and International Law' (1992) 235 *Recueil des Cours* 303; J. Fleuren, 'The Application of Public International Law by Dutch Courts' (2010) 57 *Netherlands International Law Review* 245–266; C. A. Bradley, 'Self-Execution and Treaty Duality' (2008) *Supreme Court Review* 131–182.

doctrine of European law mentioned above the criteria would pertain to the provision being sufficiently clear, precise, and unconditional).[103] The standards applied by monist domestic legal systems for finding whether a treaty provision is self-executing vary to some extent.

The early leading case of the U.S. Supreme Court on the effects of treaties within the U.S. legal order, *Foster v Neilson*, first states that:

> A treaty is in its nature a contract between two nations, not a legislative act. It does not generally effect, of itself, the object to be accomplished, especially so far as its operation is infra-territorial; but is carried into execution by the sovereign power of the respective parties to the instrument.[104]

With this reasoning the court reaffirmed the classic-orthodox international law narrative that international law creates contractual rights and obligations between states but leaves the choice of means to the parties. That is the view from international law. The court then, however, continued that:

> In the United States a different principle is established. Our constitution declares a treaty to be the law of the land. It is, consequently, to be regarded in courts of justice as equivalent to an act of the legislature, *whenever it operates of itself without the aid of any legislative provision.*[105]

---

[103] Nollkaemper, *National Courts and the International Rule of Law* at 118.
[104] *Foster & Elam v Neilson*, 27 U.S. 253 (1829), 254.
[105] *Foster & Elam v Neilson*, 27 U.S. 253 (1829), 254.

The court here referred to the Supremacy Clause of the U.S. constitution, which is indicative of a monist conception of the relationship of international and domestic law and stated that '... all Treaties made, or which shall be made, under the Authority of the United States, shall be the supreme Law of the Land; and the Judges in every State shall be bound thereby, anything in the Constitution or Laws of any State to the Contrary notwithstanding'[106]. Explicitly binding judges to international treaty obligations strongly suggests that international obligations are directly applicable before domestic courts. But the court in *Foster v Neilson* qualified this internal effect of international treaties and confined it to fields where a treaty 'operates of itself and without the aid of any legislative provision'. It thereby introduced what legal doctrine and jurisprudence then developed as the (non)self-executing distinction.[107] The court also made clear, that this choice of giving internal effect to certain kinds of treaties – the self-executing kind – follows a principle established by the U.S. constitution and is not a demand of the international legal order.

What determines whether a treaty is self-executing or not? Nuances vary among domestic legal systems and

[106] Art. VI, cl. 2, The Supremacy Clause, U.S. Constitution. Justice Gray of the US Supreme Court later famously stated that '[i]nternational law is part of our law.' *The Paquete Habana*, 175 U.S. 677, 700 (1900). See L. Henkin, 'International Law as Law in the United States' (1984) 82 *Michigan Law Review* 1555–1569.

[107] J. J. Paust, 'Self-Executing Treaties' (1988) 82 *American Journal of International Law* 760–783, 766–767 (discussing the notion of self-executing as a judicial invention).

traditions. The court in *Foster v Neilson* placed emphasis on the intent of the treaty parties, which it inferred, among other things, from the wording of the treaty.[108] What further matters, across the board, is whether the provisions are sufficiently precise to be applied without further legislation.[109] That argument is oftentimes linked to the issue of intent, the argument being that insufficient precision is indicative of an intent to deny self-execution.[110] Another condition for treaties to be self-executing is typically that they confer rights on individuals and provide a cause for action. They might also be required to be more generally justiciable, in the sense that courts may meet the objectives of the treaty by way of adjudication and implementation is not solely reserved for the legislator.[111]

Saying that a treaty is self-executing has often been understood as effectively meaning that it can be enforced in domestic courts without further implementing legislation.[112] However, the United States Court of Appeals for the Ninth Circuit recently distinguished between the issue of whether a treaty provision is self-executing and whether it may be invoked before courts. Speaking on the effect of the Vienna Convention on Consular relations it found that:

---

[108] See L. Henry, 'When Is a Treaty Self–Executing' (1928) 27 *Michigan Law Review* 776–785.

[109] See e.g. *Sei Fujii v State of California* 38 Cal.2d 718 [1952]   [110] *Ibid.*

[111] One might well say that these different bases for recognizing or rejecting treaty provisions as self-executing are, in fact, different doctrines of self-executing treaties, see Vazquez, 'The Four Doctrines of Self-Executing Treaties'.

[112] Vazquez, 'The Four Doctrines of Self-Executing Treaties' at 695.

[f]or any treaty to be susceptible to judicial enforcement it must both confer individual rights and be self-executing. There is no question that the Vienna Convention is self-executing. As such, it has the force of domestic law without the need for implementing legislation by Congress . . . But 'the questions of whether a treaty is self-executing and whether it creates private rights and remedies are analytically distinct.' [. . .]. While a treaty must be self-executing for it to create a private right of action enforceable in court without implementing domestic legislation, all self-executing treaties do not necessarily provide for the availability of such private actions.[113]

In addition to conditions of international law being sufficiently precise, not requiring further implementing action and conferring individual rights, there are other factors which indicate whether an international legal provision should be applied directly before domestic courts (even if the above conditions are met).

That a treaty is self-executing does not necessarily mean that it creates private rights enforceable in domestic courts. One additional factor would be whether international law itself grants means to enforce international legal obligations. Thus, in the already mentioned WTO dispute *US – Section 301 Trade Act*, the panel indicated that the existence of an international dispute settlement mechanism speaks against

---

[113] *Cornejo v County of San Diego* 504 F3d 853 (9th Cir 2007); see in further detail C. M. Vazquez, 'Treaties as Law of the Land: The Supremacy Clause and the Judicial Enforcement of Treaties' (2008) 122 *Harvard Law Review* 599–695; Nollkaemper, *National Courts and the International Rule of Law* at 122.

domestic applicability.[114] Conversely, however, as André Nollkaemper notes, if an international agreement sets up obligations that are enforceable domestically, then there is arguably at least a presumption that those obligations are sufficiently precise and complete.[115]

With respect to the relationship in monist legal systems of international law to the law of domestic origin (i.e. questions of 'rank') it is important to note that in spite of a generally monist stance, it is common practice to transpose international law by way of statutes or through executive action (to the extent that it is authorised by the legislature to do so) to give it the status of domestic law. While the same considerations as to the rank of international law then apply to these systems, it is more in line with the tradition of monist thinking that the general *lex posterior* rule would not apply (model A rather than B in the matrix above). Thus, even if international law were to 'only' enjoy the rank of a statute, it could not simply be set aside by a later statute.

For instance, in Austria, which blends dualist with monist features while moving further towards monism,[116]

---

[114] Panel Report, *US – Section 301 Trade Act*, WT/DS 152/R, 22 December 1999; see Nollkaemper, *National Courts and the International Rule of Law* at 34. More generally on the relevance of an international dispute settlement mechanism, B. I. Bonafé, 'Direct Effect of International Agreements in the EU Legal Order: Does It Depend on the Existence of an International Dispute Settlement Mechanism?', in E. Cannizzaro, P. Palchetti and R. A. Wessel (eds.), *International Law as Law of the European Union* (The Hague: Martinus Nijhoff, 2012) 229–248.

[115] Nollkaemper, *National Courts and the International Rule of Law* at 127.

[116] Stone Sweet and Keller, *A Europe of Rights* at 684.

later statutory legislation cannot contradict certain international treaties. Furthermore, in the Netherlands, with a very
strong monist tradition (coming close to the ideal case of
model A), international treaties can even supervene, subject
to a special parliamentary procedure, the Dutch Constitution.[117] Even if not approved by such procedure, the Dutch
Constitution provides that '[s]tatutory regulations in force in
the Kingdom shall not be applicable if such application is in
conflict with provisions of treaties that are binding on all
persons.'[118] The *lex posterior* rule is suspended for those
treaties. Other countries equally treat *certain* international
treaties at the level of statutes but provide that they still trump
later statutory legislation.

Among the ASEAN Member States, the law and practice of Vietnam might best be placed within the tradition of
monist legal systems.[119] Where international agreements are
sufficiently precise and meet the conditions of being self-
executing, they can be applied directly without a legislative act
of incorporation. Elements of the WTO Agreements were thus
deemed directly applicable – by a parliamentary resolution,
interestingly – and thus replaced domestic provisions.[120]

---

[117] Art. 91(3) Dutch Constitution.
[118] Art. 94 Dutch Constitution. See in detail A. Nollkaemper, 'The
Netherlands', in D. Sloss (ed.), *The Role of Domestic Courts in Treaty
Enforcement: A Comparative Study* (Cambridge: Cambridge University
Press, 2009) 326–369.
[119] L.-A. T. Nguyen and J. Freeman, ASEAN ITL Country Report on
Vietnam at 10.
[120] Resolution No. 71/2006/QH11, see Nguyen and Freeman, Country
Report on Vietnam at 17.

Moreover, Article 6(1) of the 2005 Treaty Law of Vietnam contains a clear rule that resolves potential conflict between international and domestic law in favour of international law: 'in cases where a legal document and a treaty to which . . . Vietnam is a party, contains different provisions on the same matter, the provisions of the treaty shall prevail.'[121]

More so than other legal systems of ASEAN Member States, the Philippine legal order combines features of monism and dualism. It classifies treaties according to the mode of admission (formal treaties, executive agreements, treaties recognized under the incorporation clause) and ranks them, by default, on an equal level with statues.[122] That is typically the case for economic agreements. In the relationship between statutes, the *lex posterior* principle applies even if this would lead to a breach of international law.[123] Some treaty norms are however accorded a higher rank than statutes and are in this sense 'constitutionalised'. That was the case for the International Covenant on Civil and Political Rights (ICCPR), which was given a quasi-constitutional effect during the interregnum period of the revolutionary government in 1986.[124]

---

[121] The Law on Conclusion, Accession to and Implementation of Treaties, passed on 14 June 2005, by the 11th National Assembly of the Socialist Republic of Vietnam at its 7th session.

[122] D. Desierto, ASEAN ITL, Country Report on The Philippines at 74–6, with reference to *Philip Morris Inc. et al. v The Court of Appeals et al.*, G.R. No. 91332, July 16, 1993.

[123] D. Desierto, ASEAN ITL, Country Report on The Philippines at 77, 105, with reference to *Secretary of Justice v Hon. Ralph C. Lantion, Presiding Judge, Regional Trial Court of Manila, Branch 25, et al.*, G.R. No. 139465, January 18, 2000 (en banc).

[124] D. Desierto, ASEAN ITL, Country Report on The Philippines at 76.

Remarkably, under the 1987 Constitution both the ICCPR and the Universal Declaration of Human Rights (UDHR) are sources of actionable legal rights for individuals. The Philippine Supreme Court recognized these norms as 'generally accepted principles of international law that form part of the law of the land' under the Incorporation Clause of the 1987 Constitution.[125]

5.6 Usual mixtures

Since so much ultimately turns on the kind of international agreements, on the practice of law-applying authorities, on international law's indirect effect, rather than the formal status of international law (if codified at all), distinguishing dualist and monist legal loses a large part of its heuristic value.[126] Moreover, domestic legal systems typically combine elements of both ideal type monist and dualist systems. There is no (monist) legal system that would treat *all* international treaties as directly applicable domestically. Conversely, virtually all (dualist) legal systems grant that even unincorporated international treaties can have *some* legal effect internally. In addition, domestic constitutions oftentimes leave a lot of interpretative space for the practice of courts, and other law-applying authorities more generally, to shape how a

---

[125] D. Desierto, ASEAN ITL, Country Report on The Philippines at 84, with reference to *BAYAN et al. v Eduardo Ermita et al.,* G.R. Nos. 169838, 169848, 169881, April 25, 2006 (en banc).

[126] For an overview of the usual overlaps also see Shelton, 'Introduction' at 4–5.

domestic legal order relates to international law. It might well be that what really matters are the attitudes among the respective domestic communities of interpreters.[127] In this section we, therefore, largely let go of the monist/dualist distinction and instead highlight the overall effect that external agreements show by virtue of (a) how they are taken into account in interpretation, and (b) how their effect might depend on whether they set up reciprocal relations between states, between states and citizens or between private parties.

5.6.1 Effects on interpretation

Regardless of whether a constitutional order shows primarily features of monism and dualism and thus to a large extent independent of the role of the legislature in mediating the relationship between international and municipal law, almost all domestic legal orders contain a variation of the principle that domestic statues should be interpreted in conformity with international law.

Typically a principle along the lines of a presumption of consistency emanates from case law and legal practice. But some domestic legal orders, such as that of South Africa, enshrine such a demand even in their constitution. Section 233 of the South African Constitution of 1996 obligates domestic courts to 'prefer any reasonable interpretation of legislation that is consistent with international law over any

---

[127] D. Sloss, 'Domestic Application of Treaties', in D. Hollis (ed.), *The Oxford Guide to Treaties* (Oxford: Oxford University Press, 2012) 379–388 (distinguishing 'nationalist' from 'transnationalist' attitudes).

alternative interpretation that is inconsistent with international law'. In addition, Section 39.1.b of the Constitution requires that any interpretation of the South African Bill of Rights 'must consider international law'.[128] Other constitutions contain similar provisions.[129]

It is in this vein that international law comes to bear on European law – understood here as an autonomous (municipal) legal order distinct from international law – even if it is not directly effective. The predominant reading of European Law, which grew out of international law into an autonomous municipal legal order, has been that it is a monist legal order. Case law has for instance affirmed that international agreements form an integral part of the legal order of the EU the moment they enter into force.[130] But that

---

[128] See in detail J. Dugard, South Africa, in D. Sloss (ed.), *The Role of Domestic Courts in Treaty Enforcement: A Comparative Study* (Cambridge Unviersity Press, 2009) 448–475.

[129] For an overview of the European Context see Stone Sweet and Keller, *A Europe of Rights*.

[130] Case 104/81, *Kupferberg*, [1982] ECR 3641, para 13. See also ECJ, Case 181/73, *Haegeman*, [1974] ECR 449, para 5; ECJ, Case C-386/08, Brita, [2010] ECR (Judgment of 25 February 2010, para 39; see Kuijper, '"It Shall Contribute to . . . the Strict Observance and Development of International Law. . ." The Role of the Court of Justice', 592–593; E. Cannizzaro, P. Palchetti, and R. A. Wessel (eds.), *International Law as Law of the European Union* (The Hague: Martinus Nijhoff, 2011); G. de Búrca, 'The European Court of Justice and the International Legal Order After Kadi' (2010) 51 *Harvard International Law Journal* 1–49; K. Lenaerts, 'Direct applicability and direct effect of international law in the EU legal order', in I. Govaere et al. (eds.), *The European Union in the world. Essays in Honour of Marc Maresceau* (Leiden: Brill, 2014) 45–64.

does not exhaust the issue of direct effect, which, as discussed above, hinges on further conditions.

Leaving those issues of direct effect aside, we turn to international law's indirect effect within the EU legal Order. In fact, it seems that a lot of arguments supporting such kind of indirect effect are driven by a desire to offset the apparent defect that there is no direct effect. When important external agreements such as the GATT and other WTO agreements are not directly applicable, forms of *indirect* effect matter all the more. EU law has set-up the principle of consistent interpretation, demanding that internal EU law be interpreted in light of the EU's external agreements that are not directly effective.[131] As Piet Eeckhout notes, 'EU Courts rarely hesitate to make use of consistent interpretation for the purpose of applying GATT and WTO law.'[132]

When EU legislation shows interpretative discretion, such discretion should be used so as to give preference to an interpretation that renders the legislation consistent with external agreements:

> When the wording of secondary Community legislation is open to more than one interpretation, preference should be given as far as possible to the interpretation which renders the provision consistent with the Treaty. Likewise, an implementing regulation must, if possible, be given an interpretation consistent with the basic regulation (see Case

---

[131] See in further detail on the 'power of consistent interpretation', Nollkaemper, *National Courts and the International Rule of Law* at 145.

[132] P. Eeckhout, *EU External Relations Law* (Oxford University Press, 2011) 356, with further references to case law.

C-90/92 *Dr Tretter* v *Hauptzollamt Stuttgart-Ost* [1993] ECR I-3569, paragraph 11). Similarly, the primacy of international agreements concluded by the Community over provisions of secondary Community legislation means that such provisions must, so far as is possible, be interpreted in a manner that is consistent with those agreements.[133]

An interesting scenario where the principle of consistent interpretation became relevant concerns the application of an EU regulation that establishes common rules for exports, which, among other things, prohibited quantitative export restrictions.[134] The question arose whether the regulation also extended to national licensing requirements for exports of dual-use goods. The ECJ answered that question in the affirmative with the support of Article XI GATT, which expresses a prohibition of quantitative export restrictions in very broad and encompassing terms.[135]

In contrast to the lack of hesitation on the part of the ECJ to give indirect effect to WTO agreements by way of interpretation, the Court does not readily rely on international judicial decisions, especially where there is a separate line of EU cases on a certain subject, such as that of anti-dumping regulations.[136]

---

[133] Case C-61/94 *Commission v Germany* [1996] ECR I-3989, para 52.

[134] Regulation 2603/69, Article1. See Eeckhout, *EU External Relations Law* at 356.

[135] Case C-70/94 *Werner v Germany* [1995] ECR I-3189, para 23 and Case C-83/94 *Leifer and Others* [1995] ECR I-3231, para 24.

[136] See Case C-351/04 *Ikea Wholesale v Commission of Customs & Exercise* [2007] ECR I-7723; see, in further detail on the effect of international litigation on EU law, Eeckhout, *EU External Relations Law* at 365–374.

In EU law, the principle of consistent interpretation is afforded general application. It need not be shown that the EU law at issue implements international law for the principle to become relevant. All the same, if implementing acts are at issue, the principle is of special relevance. The ECJ thus found that Community legislation had to be interpreted consistently with international law, *in particular* where its provisions are intended to specifically give effect to an international agreement concluded by the Community.[137] At the same time, there is an outright exception to the general rule that the WTO agreements do not have direct effect. Namely, when the EU intends to implement WTO agreements and explicitly refers to it, then the ECJ does review the legality of EU law against those agreements. That is known as the principle of implementation.[138]

The practice of ASEAN Member States with regard to giving effect to international law where there is leeway to do so in the interpretation of domestic law is mixed. Malaysia, to date, knows no case where an interpretation was supported along the lines of the *Charming Betsy* doctrine or where a presumption of consistency has been applied.[139] But there is a variation of this theme, namely, a presumption that Parliament does not intend to legislate in breach of international law.[140] With respect to Singapore, Section 9A of the

---

[137] Case C-428/08, *SGAE v Rafael Hotels SA* [2006] ECR I-11519, para 35.
[138] See Eeckhout, *EU External Relations Law*, at 361–362.
[139] Alias and Lutchman, ASEAN ITL Project at 35.
[140] *Ibid.* at 36, with reference to *Salomon v Commissions of Customs and Excise* [1967] 2 QB 116 (CA) per Lord Diplock; *R. v Secretary of State for*

Interpretation Act on purposive interpretation provides that ambiguous legislation shall generally be interpreted first in conformity with domestic law and then in light of Singapore's international obligations. International law comes into view earlier, however, if the legislation connects to international instruments, if it incorporates such instruments or otherwise uses similar language.[141] Furthermore, Singapore follows England and other common law countries in upholding the presumption that domestic legal instruments are consistent with treaty obligations. This also bears on interpretative discretion.[142]

While the Singapore courts will try to read domestic law to be consistent with international law, other factors, such as constitutional text and history, might pull into the opposite direction, nullifying the indirect effect of international law. In *Yong Vui Kong v PP,* the Court of Appeal agreed that 'domestic law, including the Singapore Constitution, should, as far as possible, be interpreted consistently with Singapore's international legal obligations.'[143] However, international law was still subject to domestic law and in this case, the constitutional text and constitutional history precluded an attempt to interpret Article 9 of the Singapore Constitution ('No one shall be deprived of life or personal liberty save in accordance with law') against the standards of Article 5 of the UDHR ('No one

the Home Department, Ex Parte Brind [1991] 1 AC 696 (HL) per Lord Bridge.

[141] E. Tan, Country Report on Singapore at 26–27.

[142] *The Sahand* [2011] 2 SLR 1093; Singaporean case following UK case: *ex p Brind* [1991] 1 AC 696.

[143] *Yong Vui Kong v PP* [2010] 3 SLR 489 at 519 [59].

shall be subjected to torture or to cruel, inhuman or degrading treatment or punishment'). Article 5 UDHR could not be read into the meaning of 'law' in Article 9 of the Constitution. In this case itself, the mandatory death penalty was being challenged as a form of inhumane punishment. The constitutional text contains no such prohibition, even though a study of constitutional history showed that a clause similar to Article 5 UDHR was considered by a Constitutional Commission in 1966, but ultimately not included in the text. The apex Court of Appeal refused to 'legislate new rights' under the guise of constitutional interpretation.[144] New rights would have to be the product of parliamentary processes or constitutional amendment.

This goes to supporting the overall dualist stance of the Singaporean legal order, also when it comes to issues of human rights. That stance further holds with regard to customary international law and even international *jus cogens*. With respect to customary international law, Singapore courts have applied a dualist approach based on the transformation doctrine by which rules of customary international law do not have domestic effect unless judicially recognised and adopted. The apex Court of Appeal held in *Yong Vui Kong v Public Prosecutor* [2010] 3 SLR 489 at [91] that a rule of customary international law, which, in any event, must be clearly established, would not be part of Singapore law 'until and unless it has been applied as or definitively declared to be part of domestic law by a domestic court'. In the subsequent case of *Yong Vui Kong v Public Prosecutor* [2015] SGCA 11 the Court

---

[144] *Yong Vui Kong v Public Prosecutor* [2010] 3 SLR 489 at [59].

of Appeal considered whether caning constituted torture. It did not deny that the prohibition against torture was a *ius cogens* norm, noting that unanimous recognition by all states was not necessary to qualify a norm as peremptory in nature, as a "very large majority" of states would suffice. However, owing to Singapore's dualist approach towards international law, peremptory norms were not automatically incorporated into domestic law nor did they take precedence over domestic law in the event of an inconsistency between the two. The Court of Appeal specifically rejected the argument that a *ius cogens* norm where it applied domestically, could overturn inconsistent legislation, because of its status as an embodiment of fundamental international values from which state derogation is not permitted.[145] The Court stated:

> The fact that peremptory norms admit of no derogation in the international sphere where relations between states are concerned, says nothing about what the position should be in the domestic sphere. Under the dualist theory of international law, there is no reason why the elevation of a particular norm to the highest status under one legal system (international law) should automatically cause it to acquire the same status and take precedence over the laws that exist in another legal system (domestic law). The two systems remain separate and a court operating in the domestic system is obliged to apply domestic legislation in the event of an irreconcilable conflict between it and international law. It may well be that the consequence of this is that a state that has enacted a law that is contrary to

[145] *Yong Vui Kong v Public Prosecutor* [2015] SGCA 11 at [34]–[35].

an applicable rule of international law is in breach of its international obligations. That alone does not invalidate the domestic legislation in question.[146]

It noted that if an international tribunal were considering an international law matter, a state would not be able to rely on its domestic legislation as a defence to its breach of international law. After examining the drafting history of the Vienna Convention on the Law of Treaties, the Court of Appeal concluded that the concept of ius cogens at its inception 'was meant to govern the international relations between states, and there was no suggestion that it would also have some special or extraordinary effect at the intra-state level.'[147]

5.6.2 *Kinds of agreements*

In addition to granting indirect effect, constitutional orders converge on treating specific kinds of external agreements differently. In further examining the specific legal practice of domestic courts while letting go of any attempt to distinguish legal systems along the lines of monism and dualism, David Sloss finds that domestic courts converge on treating different kinds of agreements differently. He shows persuasively that domestic courts are reluctant to apply and give effect to *horizontal* treaty provisions. Such 'horizontal provisions' resonate with the classic international law paradigm of inter-state relations and may be exemplified by boundary treaties, for instance. In contrast, and this is where attitudes and

---

[146] *Ibid.* at 35.   [147] *Ibid.* at 36.

explicit constitutional choices have greatest explanatory force, domestic courts do oftentimes give effect to *vertical* treaty provisions that deal with the relationship between individuals and state power. Human rights instruments would be a clear example for this kind of agreements. In addition, domestic courts generally converge on giving direct effect to what Sloss terms *transnational* treaty provisions that pertain to the actions of private parties. The 1958 Convention on the Recognition and Enforcement of Foreign Arbitral Awards ('New York'-Convention)[148] would fall into this category.

5.7 Law and policy considerations

Since many domestic legal orders leave considerable space for legal practice to shape how domestic law relates to international law, it is important to spell out the policy considerations that speak for or against giving direct effect to international treaties.

The analysis by John H. Jackson continues to offer a nuanced overview in this regard.[149] To start off, it speaks in favour of direct effect that international norms not be transformed, which saves costs of parliamentary procedures (but this may come at the price of loss of legitimacy). In fact, domestic systems that give direct effect to at least some

---

[148] Sloss, 'Domestic Application of Treaties' at 376–379

[149] J. H. Jackson, 'Status of Treaties in Domestic Legal Systems: A Policy Analysis' (1992) 86 *American Journal of International Law* 310–340. See also Keller, *Rezeption des Völkerrechts*, at 15; J. H. Jackson and A. O. Skyes, *Implementing the Uruguay Round* (Oxford: Clarendon Press, 1997) 461.

treaties typically provide for a stronger role of parliament in the making of that treaty. Either the parliament has a stronger role beforehand in relation to the executive, or it intervenes after a treaty has entered into force. Notably, one does not necessarily exclude the other. What matters further is that giving direct effect allows state organs to play a greater role in the development of international law.[150] One reason, which has fallen out of memory in many present debates, is that granting direct effect would make states better 'world citizens'. Breaches of international law would be less likely. This was, in fact, historically one of the main reasons for the Supremacy Clause in the U.S. Constitution.[151]

Reasons against direct effect include the fact that international law at times lacks the requisite democratic legitimacy. A possible deficit might then be confronted by interjecting parliamentary legislation before international law can become operative domestically.[152] The legitimacy of such a parliamentary intervention might suffer, however, from its ex-post character and from the fact that international obligations do already that leave little room for democratic

---

[150] Nollkaemper, *National Courts and the International Rule of Law*.

[151] Vazquez, 'Treaties as Law of the Land' 613–619.

[152] This was in fact what the Malaysian Court of Appeal stated in *AirAsia Berhad v Rafizah Shima Binti Mohamad Aris*, Civil No. B-02-2751-11/ 2012 (finding that CEDAW lacked the force of law until enacted by legislation; the CA said this was necessary to serve as a ' democratic check', to mitigate the lack of 'direct participation of parliament in treaty-making'. Treaties had to be incorporated as legislators 'may regard it necessary to tailor the treaty, through an act of transformation, to match domestic circumstances'. [para 52]).

deliberation.[153] Other reasons against direct effect have already been mentioned in the conditions for treaty provisions to be found self-executing; namely, that they must be sufficiently precise and generally justiciable. Furthermore, there is an argument as to which domestic organ should have the prerogative on the question of how to treat international law: the state executive or the courts.[154] Direct effect would, of course, strengthen the courts in relation to the executive.

Further arguments can be distilled from the extensive debate surrounding the implementation of WTO law and its internal effect or, usually, the lack thereof.[155] In addition to the arguments already mentioned, this context has highlighted the importance of reciprocity. It would be to the disadvantage of one WTO Member State to give direct effect to a treaty provision of trade agreements while others do not. Among

[153] A. von Bogdandy and I. Venzke, 'In Whose Name? An Investigation of International Courts' Public Authority and Its Democratic Justification' (2012) 23 *European Journal of International Law* 7–41, at 20–21.

[154] The question of whether the courts or executives are better suited to contribute to the (legitimate) development of international law lies at the core of scholarly debates, see E. Benvenisti, 'Reclaiming Democracy: The Strategic Uses of Foreign and International Law by National Courts' (2008) 102 *American Journal of International Law* 241–274 (arguing that domestic courts are well suited to develop internatinal law and, in fact, contribute to democratic legitimation in this process); K. F. Gärditz, 'Die Legitimation der Justiz zur Völkerrechtsfortbildung' (2008) 47 *Der Staat* 381–409 (arguing the opposite).

[155] Jackson and Skyes, *Implementing the Uruguay Round*; A. von Bogdandy, 'Legal Effects of World Trade Organization Decisions within European Union Law: A Contribution to the Theory of the Legal Acts of International Organizations and the Action for Damages under Article 288(2) EC' (2005) 39 *Journal of World Trade* 45–66.

other things, the executive might use some of its leverage in negotiating settlements. Conversely, Ulrich Petersmann has been an adamant advocate of giving direct effect to (most) economic agreements in order to overcome protectionism and to effectively realise the trade opportunities of private market actors.[156] The reasons against such a move, it is submitted, weigh more heavily.[157]

The specific context of ASEAN, then, may highlight one remaining factor that is connected to the argument about reciprocity and shows its flipside. In the absence of a general claim to direct effect, the different ways in which domestic constitutions treat international law, including ASEAN external agreements, may give rise to asymmetries. Whereas some Member States might recognise a treaty as self-executing and give it direct effect, others might not. The practical implications of such dissonance appear clearly in light of the example of trade law and from the perspective of a third party. With increasing economic integration – and at least when moving from a free trade area to a customs union without internal tariffs – an external producer can enter the integrated market in any Member State of its choosing. If it has the opportunity to directly challenge obstructive and illegal measures of one country against international trade obligations but not similar measures in another country, he will inevitably channel his

---

[156] E.-U. Petersmann, 'The Judicial Task of Administering Justice in Trade and Investment Law and Adjudication' (2012) 4 *Journal of International Dispute Settlement* 5–28.

[157] For a recent overview see H. Ruiz Fabri, 'Is There a Case – Legally and Politically – for Direct Effect of WTO Obligations?' (2014) 25 *European Journal of International Law* 151–173.

exports through that first country, which may be forced through its courts to set aside or suspend the obstructive and illegal measures.

Such asymmetry is certainly not viable in the long run. It might also collide with another important principle underpinning the ASEAN Charter, that of 'ASEAN centrality'. Together with strongly worded obligations of membership, the principle of ASEAN centrality, which is mentioned in different sections in the Charter, supports and demands a more unitary stance of ASEAN in relation to its external agreements and in relation to third parties. The reading of external agreements as mere plurilateral agreements, without taking into account that some of the parties together form ASEAN, overlooks this central aspiration of ASEAN and this key principle of the Charter. A reading of external agreements as joint ASEAN agreements rectifies this drawback.

The following section uses the example of the Convention to Eliminate All Forms of Discrimination Against Women (CEDAW) to illustrate how ASEAN countries treat international law. We opt for CEDAW because all ASEAN Member States are parties to the Convention. Its implementation and later practice offers a repository for insight and illustration. We use CEDAW as proxy for gauging ASEAN Members' stance towards international law in light of the relative scarcity of further material in that regard.

Chapter 6

Case study on the convention to eliminate all forms of discrimination against women

As all ASEAN states are parties to the *Convention on the Elimination of All Forms of Discrimination against Women* (CEDAW)[1], it is a useful case study on how ASEAN states implement their international legal obligations within the domestic legal framework. Since it dates back to 1979, there is also more practice to draw on for a study of its internal effects, even if it entered into force at different stages for ASEAN Member States.

It thus offers a repository of insight in a matter that is otherwise difficult to grasp. We do not yet have sufficiently evolved case-studies on the internal effects of ASEAN plurilateral agreements. By proxy, we thus study the implementation of CEDAW. A caveat pertains to the fact that the potentially intrusive and transformative reach of CEDAW has been truncated by reservations.[2] For example, contrary to Article 16 CEDAW, countries like Malaysia and Indonesia

---

[1] 1249 UNTS 13, adopted on 18 December 1979 by GA Res 34/180, entered into force 3 September 1981, U.N. Doc A/RES/34/180,1979.

[2] See generally S. Linton, 'ASEAN States, Their Reservations to Human Rights Treaties and the Proposed ASEAN Commission on Women and Children' (2008) 30 *Human Rights Quarterly* 436–493.

by dint of Muslim religious law permit polygamous marriages subject to certain conditions such as court permission.[3]

Overall, the international obligations of CEDAW may be implemented in a variety of ways, such as through the form of hortatory aspirational guidelines (a form of domestic soft law), as part of a general programme or policy administered by general or dedicated agencies, or as justiciable rights within individualized adjudicative or quasi-judicial processes. As the Malaysian Court of Appeal noted in *AirAsia Berhad v Rafizah Shima Binti Mohamad Aris*, '[e]ach State decides how best to achieve its implementation. The CEDAW Committee has no enforcement authority; it can only make recommendations highlighting areas where more progress is needed in a particular country.'[4]

Article 2 CEDAW lists the vehicles by which the obligations undertaken by state parties may be satisfied. Notably, this includes both legal and non-legal methods:

> States Parties condemn discrimination against women in all its forms, agree to pursue by all appropriate

---

[3] E.g. in Malaysia: The court will only grant permission if it is satisfied that the proposed marriage is just and necessary, having regard to such circumstances as sterility, physical infirmity, physical unfitness for conjugal relations, wilful avoidance of an order for restitution of conjugal rights or insanity on the part of the existing wife or wives. The court must be also be satisfied that the man will be able to support all his wives and dependents, and that he will be able to treat them equally and such intended marriage will not cause harm to the present wife/s. See Paras 403–406, Combined Initial and Second Periodic Reports: Malaysia, CEDAW/C/MYS/102 (12 April 2004).

[4] Civil No. B-02-2751-11/2012 (Malaysia Court of Appeal) at [34].

means and without delay a policy of eliminating discrimination against women and, to this end, undertake:

(a) To embody the principle of the equality of men and women in their national constitutions or other appropriate legislation if not yet incorporated therein and to ensure, through law and other appropriate means, the practical realization of this principle;

(b) To adopt appropriate legislative and other measures, including sanctions where appropriate, prohibiting all discrimination against women;

(c) To establish legal protection of the rights of women on an equal basis with men and to ensure through competent national tribunals and other public institutions the effective protection of women against any act of discrimination;

(d) To refrain from engaging in any act or practice of discrimination against women and to ensure that public authorities and institutions shall act in conformity with this obligation;

(e) To take all appropriate measures to eliminate discrimination against women by any person, organization or enterprise;

(f) To take all appropriate measures, including legislation, to modify or abolish existing laws, regulations, customs and practices which constitute discrimination against women;

(g) To repeal all national penal provisions which constitute discrimination against women.

The practice of implementing CEDAW within ASEAN Member States in fact reflects this wide scope of options.

6.1 Status of treaty law within domestic legal orders

Some countries, such as Cambodia and the Philippines, lean towards granting international human rights instruments direct effect and a high rank domestically. Article 31 of the Cambodian constitution states that '[t]he Kingdom of Cambodia shall recognize and respect human rights as stipulated in the United Nations Charter, the Universal Declaration of Human Rights, the covenants and conventions related to human rights, women's and children's rights.' The legislative body, the Assembly, 'shall approve or annul treaties or international conventions' (Article 90) which shall be signed and ratified by the King (Article 26). It is silent on the hierarchical status of international law within the domestic legal orders and does not provide clear guidance on cases when international law conflicts with domestic norms. Cambodia in its initial report to CEDAW stated that 'no provision of the Constitution and laws of the Kingdom of Cambodia contradict the principle of human rights as enshrined in the International Instruments.' That is, international covenant principles take precedence over domestic law.[5] Where national laws do embody CEDAW principles, 'the court uses the principles in the convention as a base'.[6]

---

[5] Combined Initial, Second and Third Periodic Reports of State Parties: Cambodia, CEDAW/C/KHM/1–3, (11 February 2004), paras 38, 49.

[6] CEDAW/C/KHM/Q/1–3/Add.1 (4 Jan 2006), Responses to the list of issues and questions for consideration of the combined initial, second and third periodic report: Cambodia (Question 2).

The Philippine Constitution of 1987 adopts under Article II (Declaration of Principles and State Policies) Section 2 'the generally accepted principles of international law as part of the law of the land'. This serves to orient the constitutional order towards compliance with international law. While there appear to be conflicting judicial authorities,[7] it appears that the Philippine Supreme Court has applied international treaties directly without legislative incorporation,[8] including human rights instruments such as the Universal Declaration of Human Rights[9] and the International Covenant on Civil and Political Rights.[10] Insofar as these are a

---

[7] See *Jose Ebro III v National Labor Relations Commission et al.* G.R. No. 110187, 4 Sept 1996

[8] E.g. *General Avelino I Razon et al. v Mary Jean Tagitis* G.R. No. 182498, 3 December 2009 (applying the UN Convention on Enforced Disappearances); *Prof Merlin M Magallona v Hon Eduardo Ermita* G.R. No. 187167, 16 August 2011 (applying UNCLOS); *Edna Diago Lhuillier v British Airways* G.R. No. 171092, 15 March 2010) (applying the Convention for the Unification of Certain Rules Relating to International Transportation by Air). Article VII Section 21 of the 1987 Constitution requires the showing of prior legislative concurrence before a treaty may be applied within the domestic legal order. Article II Section 2 provides that the Philippines adopts 'the generally accepted principles of international law as part of the law of the land'.

[9] *Boris Mejoff v The Director of Prisons*, G.R. No. L-4254, 26 September 1951. In 2006, in response to questioning by the CEDAW Committee as to the status of CEDAW in the domestic order, the response was that while it could not be used 'to bring violators of discrimination against women, it can however be cited as a reference for prosecution or defense'. CEDAW/C/PHI/Q/6/Add.1 (17 May 2006).

[10] *Government of Hong Kong v Olalia* G.R. No. 153675, 19 April 2007; *Ang Ladlad LGBT Party v Commission on Elections* G.R. No. 190582, 8 April 2010.

source of law within the Philippines legal system, they are able
to act as a source of actionable legal rights and be invoked by
individuals who challenge the constitutionality or legality of
state action as contravening standards in the constitution or
treaties.[11]

In common law countries like Singapore and Malaysia,
conversely, a treaty has to be further incorporated by domestic
legislation to be given legal effect. As such, treaties are not a
source of rights or obligations within the constitutional order.[12]
In the Singapore case of the *Sahand*,[13] for instance, Quentin
Loh J stated:

[11] E.g. the Supreme Court in *BAYAN et al. v Ermita et al.* G.R. 169838,
169848, 169881, 25 April 2006 found that the government policy of
Calibrated Preemptive Response applied to restricting the right to
assembly violated both the constitution and the International Covenant
on Civil and Political Rights. Other treaties unrelated to human rights
have also been directly invoked by individuals before Philippines Courts
e.g. individuals have claimed damages against airlines under the
Convention for the Unification of Certain Rules relating to International
Transportation: *Edna Diago Lhullier v British Airways* G.R. No. 171092,
15 March 2010.

[12] F.5, Fourth Periodic Report to CEDAW Committee: Singapore,
CEDAW/C/SGP/4 (3 April 2009) 'an aggrieved party cannot invoke the
provisions of the Convention in the law courts of Singapore' as treaties
do not become party of Singapore law unless 'specifically incorporated
into the legal system'.

[13] *The Sahand* [2011] 2 SLR 1093 at [33], approving of *JH Rayner (Mincing
Lane) Ltd v Department of Trade and Industry* [1990] 2 AC 418 at 500.
The Convention of the Rights of the Child (CRC) has been cited
approvingly where its provisions such as Article 18 confirm domestic
rules such as the idea of joint parental responsibility embodied in Section
46(1) Women's Charter Cap 535, 2009 Rev Ed: see *CX v CY (minor:
custody and access)* [2005] 3 SLR(R) 690 at [26].

By virtue of Art. 38 of the Constitution of the Republic of Singapore (1985 Rev Ed, 1999 Reprint), the legislative power of Singapore is vested in the Legislature. It would be contrary to Art. 38 to hold that treaties concluded by the Executive on behalf of Singapore are directly incorporated into Singapore law, because this would, in effect, confer upon the Executive the power to legislate through its power to make treaties. Accordingly, in order for a treaty to be implemented in Singapore law, its provisions must be enacted by the Legislature or by the Executive pursuant to authority delegated by the Legislature. In so far as a treaty is not implemented by primary or subsidiary legislation, it does not create independent rights, obligations, powers, or duties. I must therefore reject [the] submission...[that] the court can directly give effect to Singapore's treaty obligations without them being implemented through legislation, as being inconsistent with the Constitution. That said, I should state unequivocally that the courts will always strive to give effect to Singapore's international obligations within the strictures of our Constitution and laws.[14]

However, an unincorporated treaty may influence how a legal provision is interpreted in cases of ambiguity.[15] Neither the

---

[14] *The Sahand* [2011] 2 SLR 1093 at [33]

[15] 'CEDAW is without doubt a treaty in force and Malaysia's commitment to CEDAW is strengthen when art 8(2) of the Federal Constitution was amended to incorporate the provision of CEDAW which is not part of the reservation, i.e. to include non-discrimination based on gender. As such, I am of the opinion that there is no impediment for the court to refer to CEDAW in interpreting Art. 8(2) of the Federal Constitution'. *Noorfadilla Ahmad Saikin v Chayed Basirun & Ors* [2012] 1 MLJ 832 at [32] Malaysian High Court (Shah Alam).

Singapore nor Malaysian constitutions refer to international law as a source of the law of the land.

6.2 Constitutional amendments and judicial enforcement

6.2.1 *Embodying treaty obligations in basic law*

While the constitutions of the ten ASEAN states all have equality clauses, none have adopted the broad definition of substantive equality in CEDAW or its conception of direct and indirect discrimination. This is a constant concern of the CEDAW Committee.[16]

Cambodia, which styles itself as 'a Kingdom with a King who shall rule according to the Constitution and to the principles of liberal democracy and pluralism' (chapter 1, Article 1 of the Constitution), for example ratified CEDAW without reservations on 15 October 1992.[17] Its constitution was adopted by a Constitutional Assembly on 21 September 1993, just after the country emerged from conflict. It reflects many of the international human rights obligations Cambodia has accepted,[18] including a general equality clause which

---

[16] E.g. CEDAW Committee, Concluding Comments: Philippines, CEDAW/C/PHI/CO/6 (25 August 2006), para 9; Concluding Comments: Singapore, CEDAW/C/SGP/CO/4/Rev.1 (5 January 2012), para 12; Concluding Comments: Thailand, CEDAW/C/THA/CO/5 (3 February 2006), para 15.

[17] Combined Initial, Second and Third Periodic Reports of State Parties: Cambodia, CEDAW/C/KHM/1–3 (11 February 2004), para 3.

[18] Article 31 of the Constitution of the Kingdom of Cambodia (1993) states that, 'The Kingdom of Cambodia shall recognize and respect human

143

prohibits, inter alia, discrimination on the basis of sex (Article 31), and also provides that '[m]en and women are equal in all fields, especially in marriage and matters of the family' (Article 45). This resonates with Article 16 CEDAW. In addition, Article 34 of the Constitution provides for equality between men and women in voting and standing as candidates for elections. To give effect to this, it has also adopted the policy to have at least one woman as deputy governor in municipal and district authorities, to ensure the involvement of women in politics and public decision-making, as Article 7 CEDAW requires. The requirement in Article 11(2) of CEDAW that state parties should take appropriate measures '[t]o prohibit, subject to the imposition of sanctions, dismissal on the grounds of pregnancy or of maternity leave...' is also reflected in Article 46 of the Constitution.[19] Article 39 empowers citizens to make complaints against any breach of the law or abuse of their rights by state officials, which falls within the jurisdictional competence of the courts. This includes women victimised by violation of their rights or the use of violence against them.[20]

rights as stipulated in the Charter of the United Nations, the Universal Declaration of Human Rights and the Covenants and Conventions related to human rights, women's and children's rights.'

[19] 'A woman shall not lose her job because of pregnancy. Women shall have the right to take maternity leave with full pay and with no loss of seniority or other social benefits.'

[20] Combined Initial, Second and Third Periodic Reports of State Parties: Cambodia, CEDAW/C/KHM/1–3, (11 February 2004), paras 80–81.

While the 2008 Constitution of Myanmar formally prohibits sex discrimination,[21] the CEDAW Committee has expressed concern that this does not protect substantive equality in accordance with the definition of discrimination (direct/indirect, public/private) in Article 1 CEDAW.[22] It also has pointed out that the Constitution itself recognises sex-based discrimination.[23]

While Thai law does not contain a clear definition of discrimination, Thailand has stated that it 'has agreed to apply the definition' contained in Article 1 CEDAW.[24] The CEDAW Committee in 2006 urged that this be incorporated in its Constitution or Gender Equality bill then being drafted,[25] and this recommendation was heeded to.[26]

---

[21] Article 348: 'The Union shall not discriminate any citizen of the Republic of the Union of Myanmar, based on race, birth, religion, official position, status, culture, sex and wealth.' Notably, Myanmar became a state party to CEDAW in 1997.

[22] CEDAW Committee Concluding Observations: Myanmar, CEDAW/C/MMR/CO/3 (7 November 2008) at para 8.

[23] Article 352: 'The Union shall, upon specified qualifications being fulfilled, in appointing or assigning duties to civil service personnel, not discriminate for or against any citizen of the Republic of the Union of Myanmar, based on race, birth, religion and sex. However, nothing in this Section shall prevent appointment of men to the positions that are suitable for men only.' Para 10, CEDAW Concluding Observations: Myanmar, CEDAW/C/MMR/CO/3 (7 November 2008).

[24] Combined Fourth and Fifth Periodic Report: Thailand, CEDAW/C/THA/4–5, (24 June 2004), para 25.

[25] CEDAW Committee, Concluding Observations: Thailand CEDAW/C/THA/CO/5 (3 February 2006) para 16.

[26] Section 4(3) of the Thai Promotion of Opportunity and Gender Equality Bill reads: 'Unfair gender discrimination means any illegal commission

6.2.2 Use of treaty norms to inform the formulation of fundamental laws

While Cambodia has not yet defined 'discrimination against women' in its domestic laws, Article 31 of its Constitution reflects a commitment to accept the definition stipulated in CEDAW as the basis for all legal documents and policy developments to promote equality between men and women.[27] Indeed, Article 31 is said to 'demonstrate' that Cambodia recognizes and respects CEDAW and complies with the definition of the term 'discrimination against women' in CEDAW.[28]

Malaysia acceded to CEDAW on 5 July 1995 and on 1 August 2001, it gave effect to Article 2(a) by expanding its constitutional prohibition against discrimination contained in Article 8(2) of the Federal Constitution of Malaysia (1957).[29] In its prior incarnation, Article 8(2) prohibited

or omission which is a direct or indirect distinction, exclusion or restriction on the basis of sex, with or without intention; resulting in a non-recognition or inability to exercise inherent individual fundamental rights merely on the basis of sex.' See C. Foster and V. Jivan, *Gender Equality Laws: Global Good Practice and a Review of Five Southeast Asian Countries* (UNIFEM, 2009) at 106. Available at: www.snap-undp .org/lepknowledgebank/Public%20Document%20Library/Gender% 20Equality%20Laws-Global%20Good%20Practice%20and%20a% 20Review%20of%205%20SEA%20countries.pdf.

[27] Combined Initial, Second and Third Periodic Reports of State Parties: Cambodia, CEDAW/C/KHM/1–3 (11 February 2004), at paras 60–61, 63.

[28] Combined Fourth and Fifth Periodic Report: Cambodia, CEDAW/C/ KHM/4–5 (24 Sept 2011) at para 27.

[29] Text available at http://confinder.richmond.edu/admin/docs/malaysia .pdf.

'discrimination against citizens on the ground only of religion, race, descent or place of birth in any law relating to the acquisition, holding or disposition of property or the establishing or carrying on of any trade, business, profession, vocation or employment, except where the constitution otherwise expressly authorised.' It was amended[30] to include 'gender' as a basis for prohibiting non-discrimination, 'to comply with Malaysia's obligations' under CEDAW, as stated by Zahela Yusof J in *Noorfadilla Ahmad Saikin v Chayed Basirun & Ors*,[31] citing the ministerial speech accompanying the constitutional amendment bill.

The new Article 8(2) was invoked before the Malaysian courts for the first time in *Beatrice a/p A.T. Fernandez v Sistem Penerbangan Malaysia*.[32] The apex Federal Court held that Article 8(2) had no 'horizontal' reach, that is, it did not apply between private parties or contracts. The case itself involved a challenge by a former air-stewardess who had been dismissed because she was pregnant, in accordance with the terms of a collective agreement with the air carrier requiring pregnant stewardesses to resign. The Federal Court held that Article 8 could only be invoked if an applicant could show that legislation or executive action had discriminated against her as:

> Constitutional law, as a branch of public law, deals with the contravention of individual rights by the Legislature or the Executive or its agencies. Constitutional law does not extend

[30] Constitution (Amendment) (No. 2) Act 2001 (Act A1130), which came into force on 28 September 2001.
[31] [2012] 1 MLJ 832 Malaysian High Court (Shah Alam) at [18].
[32] [2005] 2 CLJ 713.

its substantive or procedural provisions to infringements of an individual's legal right by another individual. Further, the reference to the 'law' in Art. 8 of the Federal Constitution does not include a collective agreement entered into between an employer and a trade union of workmen.[33]

As such, the inclusion of a gender-based non-discrimination clause in the Malaysian constitution has limited reach in the private sphere; it would take domestic legislation. For example, in the form of a gender equality law, for such a norm to be enforceable between private parties, though they may pursue private law remedies.

It was later raised before the High Court in *Noorfadilla* where the basic complaint was that a woman's job offer was rescinded by a public authority because she was pregnant, which was unconstitutional. The Court cited the definition of 'discrimination' in Article 1 of CEDAW[34] as well as Article 11 (1)(b) which required states to take 'all appropriate measures' to eliminate gender discrimination in the field of employment. The Court noted previous judicial pronouncements, which identified the Universal Declaration of Human Rights (1984) as not being legally binding, as it was not a treaty but a General Assembly Resolution.[35] However, CEDAW was a convention and had 'the force of law', being 'binding on Member States, including Malaysia'. In addition, Malaysia had 'pledged its continued commitments to ensure that Malaysian practices

---

[33] [2005] 2 CLJ 713 at 720 e–f.
[34] [2012] 1 MLJ 832 Malaysian High Court (Shah Alam) at [20].
[35] Siti Norma FCJ in *Mohd Ezam Mohd Noor v Ketua Polis Negara* [2002] 4 MLJ 449 at p 514.

are compatible with the provision and principles of CEDAW as evidenced in the letter from the Permanent Mission of Malaysia to the Permanent Missions of the Members States of the United Nations dated 9 March 2010.[36] The judge also referenced a 'soft law' document from a conference setting forth the 1988 Bangalore Colloquium, drawing from this the principle that judges should have regard to international obligations, whether or not incorporated into domestic law, to remove ambiguity from national laws. He concluded that as it was 'the obligation of this court', it had 'no choice' but to refer to Malaysia's CEDAW obligations in defining equality and gender discrimination under Article 8(2) of the Constitution.[37] Thus in applying Articles 1 and 11 of CEDAW, the judge held that the withdrawal of the job offer because the plaintiff was pregnant was a form of gender discrimination.[38] The judge appeared to follow the approach of the Australian decision of *Minister for Immigration and Ethnic Affairs v Teoh*[39], which was applied in the Indian case of *Vishaka v State of Rajasthan.*[40] The proposition adopted was that unincorporated treaties could not be a direct source of individual rights and duties; nonetheless, such treaties could have an effect in interpretation, where constructions consistent with treaty obligations were to be preferred.[41] The High Court judge also

---

[36] [2012] 1 MLJ 832 Malaysian High Court (Shah Alam) at [24].

[37] [2012] 1 MLJ 832 Malaysian High Court (Shah Alam) at [25]–[26], [28].

[38] 'Discrimination on the basis of pregnancy is a form of gender discrimination because basic biological fact is that only woman has the capacity to become pregnant.' [32].

[39] (1995) 128 ALR 353.   [40] AIR 1997 SC 3011.

[41] [2012] 1 MLJ 832 Malaysian High Court (Shah Alam) at [29].

broadened the interpretive matrix by referring to two 'soft' non-binding documents which referred to women's rights, to which Malaysia 'is also party to'; that is the Beijing Statement of Principles of the Independence of the Judiciary in the LAWASIA Region and the Fourth World Conference on Women in Beijing.[42] Thus, international treaty law and associated soft law instruments have been referenced by Malaysian courts to fill in the content of the non-discrimination constitutional clause in Article 8(2), in relation to gender and workplace discrimination. While *Noorfadilla* was followed by a later High Court judgment which treated the Convention on the Rights of the Child (which Malaysia acceded to in 1995 but did not give effect to by way of legislation) as incorporated in the Malaysian common law[43], the current Malaysian position is confused as the Court of Appeal in *AirAsia Berhad v Rafizah Shima Binti Mohamad Aris*[44] rejected the approach in *Noorfadilla*. The Court of Appeal pointed out that CEDAW did not have the force of law in Malaysia because it had not been enacted by local legislation.[45] Thus, a woman who was dismissed from a training course for becoming pregnant was not able to invoke CEDAW to argue that the training agreement discriminated against women.

[41] [2012] 1 MLJ 832 Malaysian High Court (Shah Alam) at [29].
[42] [2012] 1 MLJ 832 Malaysian High Court (Shah Alam) at [30]–[31].
[43] *Lee Lai Ching (as the next friend of Lim Chee Zheng and on behalf of herself) v Lim Hooi Teik* [2013] 4 MLJ 272 at [30].
[44] Civil No. B-02–2751-11/2012 (Malaysia Court of Appeal).
[45] The High Court in *SIS Forum (Malaysia) v Dato' Seri Syed Hamid bin Syed Jaafar Albar (Menteri Dalam Negeri)* [2010] 2 MLJ 378 noted at [37] that the Australian case of *Teoh* had received its 'fair share of criticism',

Laos PDR acceded to CEDAW in 1981. In its amendment to the Constitution in 2003, it included specific clauses declaring that citizens 'of both genders' enjoyed equal rights 'in the political, economic, culture and social fields and in family affairs' (Article 37). This is elaborated upon in various statutes.[46] Prime Minister Decree No. 26/PM (6 Feb 2006) has specifically defined 'discrimination against women' as 'all forms of act creating division, exclusion or restriction toward women made on the basis of sex, depriving women of social respect for their rights, gender equality, human rights, freedoms in political, economic, cultural, social or any other field.'[47]

6.2.3 Specific clauses

Singapore acceded to CEDAW in 1995 but has to date not amended its constitution to include a general prohibition

and that the approach of Malaysian courts was not to directly accept norms of international law unless incorporated as part of municipal law.

[46] E.g. Article 13 of the Law on Development and Protection of Women stipulates that 'equal right of women and men means equal right to self-development. Women and men have the same value and opportunities in politics, economy, socio-culture, families, national defense and security and foreign affairs as stipulated in the Constitution and laws.' Prime Minister Decree No. 26/PM of 6 February 2006 defines 'discrimination against women' under Article 2 as: 'discrimination against women is all forms of act creating division, exclusion or restriction toward women made on the basis of sex, depriving women of social respect for their rights, gender equality, human rights, freedoms in political, economic, cultural, social or any other field.'

[47] Combined Sixth and Seventh Periodic Report: Lao PDR, Part II: Article 1 CEDAW/C/LAO/7 (30 May 2008) at 7.

against discrimination on grounds of gender. The view of the government is that the prohibition against gender discrimination is implicit in Article 12(1), which provides 'All persons are equal before the law and entitled to the equal protection of the law.'[48] That is, that Singapore laws protecting the principles of gender equality were already in place before Singapore's accession to CEDAW,[49] such that no legal reform was needed. The Indonesian Constitution 1945 (Second Amendment, 2000) also contains a general non-discrimination clause, which would encompass discrimination against women.[50]

However, Singapore did amend Article 122 of the Republic of Singapore Constitution in 2004 such that women were granted equal rights with men with respect to the nationality of their children.[51] Previously, a child born outside Singapore was granted Singapore citizenship by descent only

---

[48] Fourth Periodic Report to CEDAW Committee: Singapore, CEDAW/C/SGP/4 (3 April 2009) at para 2.4: 'Although there is no specific gender equality and anti-gender discrimination legislation in Singapore, the principle of equality of all persons before the law is enshrined in the Singapore Constitution. This provision encompasses the non-discrimination of women.'

[49] F.1, Fourth Periodic Report to CEDAW Committee: Singapore, CEDAW/C/SGP/4 (3 April 2009).

[50] Article 28 I(2) states: 'everyone is entitled to be free from discriminatory treatment on any basis and is entitled to be protected from discriminatory treatment'. Notably, Indonesia signed CEDAW on 29 July 1980 and ratified it on 24 July 1984 with Indonesian Act No. 7/1984 ratified CEDAW on 24 July 13 September 1984.

[51] Fourth Periodic Report to CEDAW Committee: Singapore, CEDAW/C/SGP/4 (3 April 2009), paras 2.3., 9.1–9.3.

if his or her father was a Singapore citizen.[52] Rendering the rule gender-neutral was presented as a 'milestone' development in the state report to the CEDAW Committee, although CEDAW was not referenced in the relevant parliamentary debates.[53]

6.3 Conforming statutes to CEDAW

One way in which treaties are implemented is where state parties take pains to ensure that domestic legislation is in conformity with treaty standards by amending existing law or enacting new laws.

State bodies may be enjoined to review existing legislation to give effect to international obligations. For example, the Indonesian government created the Office of the Minister of State for the Role of Women in 1978 which was tasked with making an inventory of laws, practices and regulations which discriminated against women and to submit proposals for legislation that needed to be enacted or amended to comply with CEDAW.[54]

---

[52] Notably, the Malaysia lodged a reservation with respect to article 9(2) CEDAW which grants women equal rights with men regarding the nationality of their children. Under Article 14 of the Federal Malaysian Constitution, a person born outside the Federation would be a citizen only if his or her father was a Malaysian.

[53] The motivation for the amendment was to serve the state objective of boosting declining birth rates: 'More foreign-born kids to get citizenship' *Straits Times* (20 April 2004) at H2; CEDAW Committee, Fourth Periodic State Reports: Singapore (3 April 2009), CEDAW//SGP/4 at para 2.2.

[54] Second and Third reports of State parties: Indonesia CEDAW/C/IDN/ 2–3, (12 February 1997) at 8.

The Royal Government of Cambodia reported abrogating all Criminal Law provisions, which discriminated against women in its initial report to the CEDAW Committee.[55] It amended its Penal Code[56] to punish acts that 'discriminate against women', as understood within the CEDAW context.[57] It contains various articles, which punish acts that discriminate against women by public sector actors. For example, Articles 267–68[58] criminalises discrimination against women in the form of a refusal to employ someone on the basis of sex.[59] Article 270[60] makes it a crime for civil servants (in the course of fulfilling their public functions) to discriminate against a person on the basis of that person's sex, denying a person the enjoyment of his or her rights.

In 2006 the Lao PDR National Assembly amended various laws including the Labour Law which equalised the

---

[55] Combined Initial, Second and Third Periodic Reports of State Parties: Cambodia, CEDAW/C/KHM/1–3, (11 February 2004) at paras 100–102.

[56] Royal Decree No. NS/RK/1109/022 dated 30 November 2009.

[57] Combined Fourth and Fifth Periodic Report: Cambodia, CEDAW/C/KHM/4–5 (24 September 2011) at para 28.

[58] 'Refusal to employ any person if such refusal to employ is based on the person's sex shall be subject to a punishment of imprisonment from one month to one year or a fine from 100,000 riel to 2 million riel.'

[59] Combined Initial, Second and Third Periodic Reports of State Parties: Cambodia, CEDAW/C/KHM/1–3, (11 February 2004), at paras 74–76.

[60] 'Acts committed by civil servants in performing their functions or in fulfilling their functions of denying anyone the enjoyment of their rights if such denial is based on the person's sex shall be subject to a punishment of imprisonment from six months to two years and a fine from 1 million riel to 4 million riel.'

retirement age for men and women.[61] To eliminate discrimination against women, for example, the Malaysian government abolished immigration regulations[62] which discriminated against Malaysian women married to foreigners, by enabling their husbands to stay in the country longer (one year, as opposed to three months).

States may seek to fulfill their international obligations under Article 2 of CEDAW by adopting general human rights legislation, comprehensive gender-equality laws or issue-specific legislation[63] which protects women against discrimination on the basis of gender.

When it concerns the adoption of general human rights legislation, we may point to the Indonesian Law No. 39 of 1999 on Human Rights which defines discrimination under Article 1(3) as follows:

> Discrimination is any limitation, harassment or exclusion, whether direct or indirect, based on human differentiation determined by religion, tribe, race, ethnicity, group, association, social status, economic status, sex, language, or political belief, that causes the reduction, deviation from, or abolition of the recognition, implementation or use of human rights and fundamental freedoms in the political,

[61] Combined Sixth and Seventh Periodic Report: Lao PDR, Part II: Article 1 CEDAW/C/LAO/7 (30 May 2008) at 8.

[62] Initial and Second Report, CEDAW Committee: Malaysia at para 73.

[63] E.g. The Cambodia MoWVA drew up a draft Law on the Prevention of Domestic Violence and the Protection of the Victims Combined Initial, Second and Third Periodic Reports of State Parties: Cambodia, CEDAW/C/KHM/1–3, (11 February 2004) at [99].

economic, legal, social, cultural, and other aspects of life, whether at the individual or collective level.

This includes discrimination against women. Article 17 guarantees women effective protection, through competent national tribunals and other public institutions, against any act of discrimination.

When it comes to specific gender equality statutes, various ASEAN states have adopted legislative measures to implement CEDAW obligations, which may encompass a comprehensive or a narrower range of substantive rights.

Three of the ten ASEAN states have adopted Gender Equality Statutes (while Indonesia, Myanmar and Thailand have formulated draft bills)[64]: Vietnam's 2006 Law on Gender Equality, Laos PDR's Law on the Protection and Development of Women 2004 and the Decree on the Implementation of the Law on the Development and Protection of Women 2006, and the Philippines' 2009 Act (Republic Act 9710) Providing for the Magna Carta of Women (MCW),[65] which is based on CEDAW provisions. Chapter 1 Section 2 (Declaration of Policy) expressly provides that the state shall eliminate discrimination against women 'in keeping with' CEDAW, and

---

[64] Indonesia: CEDAW/C/IDN/Q/6–7/Add.1 at para 28 (Responses to the list of issues and questions with regard to the consideration of the combined Sixth and Seventh Periodic Report: Indonesia), 19 January 2012. See Foster and Jivan, *Gender Equality Laws*, at 83–112.

[65] Dates of ratification/accession of CEDAW: Cambodia (1992) Indonesia (1984); Lao PDR (1981); Malaysia (1995); Myanmar (1997); Philippines (1981); Singapore (1995); Thailand (1985); Vietnam (1982) – Information available at 'CEDAW in Action in Southeast Asia' at http://cedaw-seasia .org/index.html.

requires that the state take steps to review, amend or repeal existing laws that discriminate against women. Under Section 41, the Philippines Commission of Human Rights, a constitutionally established body, upon finding a violation of any provision by a government actor, shall recommend sanctions to the Civil Service Commission and the person directly responsible shall be held liable. A private person who commits a violation is held to be directly responsible and liable to pay damages.

Vietnam adopted its 2006 Law on Gender Equality[66] to give effect to its international obligations under CEDAW. Article 5(5) defines gender discrimination as an 'act of restricting, excluding, not recognizing or not appreciating the role and position of man and woman leading to inequality between man and woman in all fields of social and family life'. Article 3 of the Vietnam Law on Gender Equality provides that the provisions of an international treaty, where inconsistent with domestic law, shall prevail. It assigns responsibilities to various government bodies to mainstream gender equality in law-making and in monitoring the implementation of these laws, and is intrusive in stipulating apparently non-justiciable duties on the family (Article 33(2): 'to educate members of the family to be responsible for sharing housework and allocating housework to members of the family in an appropriate manner'.) and on individual citizens (Article 34(3) 'to criticize and prevent any gender discriminatory acts'). Violations of gender equality under the law on

---

[66] Law No. 73/2006/Qh11 (28 Nov 2006); text available at: www.ilo.org/dyn/travail/docs/934/Law%20on%20Gender%20Equality%202006.pdf.

complaint and denunciation are to be handled by the state management agency on gender equality (Article 35(2)(c)). Those guilty of violating the law on gender equality 'shall be subject to disciplinary measures, administrative sanctions or criminal prosecutions' (Article 42(1)). Where such violations by agencies, organizations and individuals have caused damages, there is a duty to compensate for that damage in compliance with the law (Article 42(2)).

One of the specific goals of CEDAW, as embodied in Article 5, is to eliminate gender stereotypes which perpetuate gender discrimination. To this end, temporal affirmative measures may be adopted, under Article 4. For example, the Cambodian Co-Statute of Civil Servants provides that women may be given priority in selection for employment.[67] The Cambodian Royal government has decided that municipal authorities must include at least one woman in a leadership position, consonant with Article 4 CEDAW which permits temporal special measures to hasten gender equality. It also gives permanent special treatment to public servants who, when pregnant, are entitled to take three months maternity leave with full pay, as provided by the Labour Law.[68]

---

[67] Combined Initial, Second and Third Periodic Reports of State Parties: Cambodia, CEDAW/C/KHM/1–3, (11 February 2004), para 124.

[68] This Labour Law provides that (1) After giving birth, women are entitled to take 90 days maternity leave and receive half of their wage and other perquisites, if any. Women are then entitled to only perform light work for the following two months after their maternity leave; and (2) An employer is prohibited from firing women during their maternity leave or if the end of their notice period falls within their period of maternity leave.

3. CONFORMING STATUTES TO CEDAW

In order to promote the participation of women in decision-making bodies, the Cambodian government has determined that one of three village leaders must be female whereas in Village Development Committees, 40 per cent must be female.[69]

In the context of political participation, Article 65(1) of the Indonesian Law No. 12 of 2002 on General Elections calls on political parties to ensure there is at least 30 per cent women's representation in their list of candidates for the legislature.[70] No legal sanctions are provided for under the Regulations of the General Election Commission if a political party submits less than 30 per cent women candidates. The State has sanctioned a 30 per cent quota for women under Law 2/2007 regarding the Proceeding of General Elections, Law 2/2008 regarding Political Parties, and Law 10/2008 regarding General Elections.[71] Article 55 of the Indonesian Electoral Law 10/2008 which relates to elections to the House

---

[69] Para 128, Combined Initial, Second and Third Periodic Reports of State Parties: Cambodia, CEDAW/C/KHM/1–3, (11 February 2004).

[70] CEDAW/C/IDN/Q/6–7/Add.1 at para 56 (Responses to the list of issues and questions with regard to the consideration of the combined Sixth and Seventh Periodic Report: Indonesia), 19 January 2012. 'During the last National Election in 2009, the 30 per cent of quota for women participation in politics as temporary special measures was mandatory. The measure was one of the requirements for political parties to join general legislative election, according to Law on General Election. They were required to include 30 per cent of women in their proposed list of legislative candidates otherwise they could not proceed to participate in legislative election.'

[71] Combined Sixth and Seventh Periodic Reports: Indonesia CEDAW/C/IDN/6–7 (7 January 2001), para 26.

of Representatives, requires that 'at least one in every three candidates included on a political party list should be women.'[72] The Indonesian Constitutional Court has noted that while this brand of affirmative action 'is a policy which has been accepted by Indonesia, which originates from CEDAW', in the event where the Court is 'presented with a choice between the principles provided for in the 1945 Constitution and policy demands based on CEDAW, the 1945 Constitution must be prioritized'.[73]

One specific concern has been how consistency could be ensured in decentralised, strongly federal structures. As a matter of international responsibility, states are certainly responsible for the acts and policies of local administration. One of the problems arising in decentralised systems is the need of the central government to ensure consistency of local laws and policies with international obligations. In relation to CEDAW, decentralisation and regional autonomy within Indonesia[74] has given rise to the problem of the flourishing

---

[72] The Constitutional Court of Indonesia noted that the obligation in Art 55(2) of Law No. 10 of 2008 stating that for every three candidates, at least one had to be female, was a form of affirmative action and a following up to CEDAW and associated conferences like the 1995 World Conference on Women in Beijing. This was considered a form of special treatment under Article 28H(2) of the 1945 Constitution. The 30 per cent quota for women was a form of positive discrimination as well: Decision Number 22–24/PUU-VI/2008 at [3.15.1]: www.codices.coe.int/NXT/gateway.dll/CODICES/full/asi/ina/eng/ina-2008-n-004.

[73] Decision Number 22–24/PUU-VI/2008 at [3.16]: www.codices.coe.int/NXT/gateway.dll/CODICES/full/asi/ina/eng/ina-2008-n-004.

[74] Combined Sixth and Seventh Periodic Reports: Indonesia CEDAW/C/IDN/6–7 (7 January 2001).

of gender-biased perspectives based on 'narrow interpretation of religious teachings that undermine women'.[75] To that end, the Department of Law and Human Rights has issued guidelines for drafting regional by-laws to prevent contradiction with superior laws and to ensure that they are not gender-biased.[76] It has also reviewed various regional by-laws to ensure they are not discriminatory: as of 2007, it was reported that of the 5518 regional by-laws reviewed, 1406 were recommended for annulment.[77] In 2011 the Ministry of Law and Human Rights and the Ministry of Home Affairs issued a parameter on gender equality as a guideline for the formulation of by-laws after Law No. 12 of 2011 on the Formulation of Laws and Regulations.[78] The CEDAW Committee has stressed the direct responsibility of the central government to fulfill its obligations (which were in no way reduced by the decentralisation of power through autonomy schemes) towards all women within its jurisdiction, including the provincial levels.[79]

---

[75] Para 1, Combined Sixth and Seventh Periodic Reports: Indonesia CEDAW/C/IDN/6–7 (7 January 2001).

[76] Para 8, Combined Sixth and Seventh Periodic Reports: Indonesia CEDAW/C/IDN/6–7 (7 January 2001).

[77] Para 20, Combined Sixth and Seventh Periodic Reports: Indonesia CEDAW/C/IDN/6–7 (7 January 2001).

[78] Para 26, CEDAW/C/IDN/Q/6–7/Add.1 (Responses to the list of issues and questions with regard to the consideration of the combined Sixth and Seventh Periodic Report: Indonesia), 19 January 2012.

[79] Para 16, CEDAW/C/IDN/Q/6–7/Add.1 (Responses to the list of issues and questions with regard to the consideration of the combined Sixth and Seventh Periodic Report: Indonesia), 19 January 2012.

So too, Article 58 of the Cambodian Law on Administrative Management of Capital, Provinces, Cities, Districts and Khams (24 May 2008) provides that any by-law, which discriminates against an individual or a specific group of people on various grounds, including 'sex', would be invalid.

A specific question on which ASEAN Member States further diverge is whether they grant individuals an individual right to bring a claims. In Cambodia, an aggrieved individual may file a lawsuit with a court to resolve civil disputes under Article 2 of the Civil Procedure Code.

In Singapore, individuals cannot directly invoke CEDAW before Singapore courts, though judicial remedies for claims of gender discrimination contrary to Article 12 of the Constitution may be made. Under the law, some degree of redress through complaints procedures to the relevant authorities and agencies are available. Such complaints are recorded, and the agencies' responses are monitored.[80] The preference appears to be to provide for informal complaints channels within government agencies or Parliament, rather than, or in tandem with, legal remedies.[81]

---

[80] Para 2.6, Fourth Periodic Report to CEDAW Committee: Singapore, CEDAW/C/SGP/4 (3 April 2009): 'Although there is no specific gender equality and anti-gender discrimination legislation in Singapore, the principle of equality of all persons before the law is enshrined in the Singapore Constitution. This provision encompasses the non-discrimination of women.'

[81] Para 32.22, Responses to the list of issues and questions: Fourth Periodic Report: Singapore, CEDAW/C/SGP/Q/4/Add.1 (12 May 2011).

6.4 National mechanisms

ASEAN states have adopted various forms of national mechanisms to promote CEDAW norms, whether through dedicated monitoring agencies or attempts to co-ordinate and mainstream gender equality norms across ministries. These agencies oversee CEDAW obligations through promotional activities such as training sessions or through gender mainstreaming policies and guidelines, which are more exhortatory in nature than legally binding.

In Cambodia, the Ministry of Women's and Veterans' Affairs and ministerial-level Cambodia National Council for Women are charged with drawing up plans to implement human rights treaties to which Cambodia is party. Aside from CEDAW, attention is paid to related woman's rights declarations such as the Beijing Platform for Action,[82] a form of aspirational soft law which set forth a programme to promote the realization of gender equality norms. It also monitors acts of discrimination against women 'in order to draw up a principle to denounce the discrimination against women'.[83]

The Philippines Commission of Women,[84] originally established by Presidential Decree No. 633 of 1975, was

---

[82] Paras 55–56, Combined Initial, Second and Third Periodic Reports of State Parties: Cambodia, CEDAW/C/KHM/1–3, (11 February 2004).

[83] Para 87, Combined Initial, Second and Third Periodic Reports of State Parties: Cambodia, CEDAW/C/KHM/1–3, (11 February 2004).

[84] It was originally the National Commission on the Role of Filipino Women whose names altered by Republic Act 9710 (Magna Carta of Women).

charged with monitoring the implementation of CEDAW which the Philippines ratified in 1981. It adopted the Philippine Plan for Gender-Responsive Development (1995–25) as a method of implementing the 1995 Beijing Declaration and Platform for Action.

There may be difficulties in realizing gender equality where existing laws perpetuate stereotypes, contrary to Article 5 CEDAW which requires governments to eliminate gender stereotypes. Law 1/1974 regarding Marriage and Islamic Law Compilation in Indonesia still stipulates that the husband is the head of the family and the wife the homemaker. The Law also permits polygamy. In response, the Indonesian Ministry for Women Empowerment and Child Protection has sought to conduct training to broaden views about gender equality, consequent to the Presidential Instruction 9/2000 regarding Gender Mainstreaming. For example, the training provided by the Early Child Care Development training programme for parents seeks to eliminate the stereotypical notion that women are solely responsible for raising children. The government also produces gender mainstreaming guidelines for journalists and adopts the 'carrot' of giving annual awards for the best writing on gender issues.

Governments have also mandated that specific bodies monitor the activities of government bodies with respect to the principle of non-discrimination against women, as in the case of Cambodia's Ministry of Women's Affairs (MoWA), which is assisted by provincial line departments.[85] Indonesia's

---

[85] Combined Fourth and Fifth Periodic Report: Cambodia, CEDAW/C/KHM/4–5 (24 September 2011), at paras 41–42.

Ministry of Women Empowerment (MOWE) has conducted CEDAW awareness training for ministries and central as well as provincial government institutions. It has run studies with other ministries and NGOs with a view to harmonizing existing laws with CEDAW principles, in such areas as domestic violence, protecting migrant workers and trafficking of women and children. In addition, it has directed consultations in 2002 with other ministries to formulate gender mainstreaming policies and strategies. The Cambodian government has adopted a policy of holistically incorporating gender mainstreaming into all spheres of life, and has established in twenty-six ministries and institutions Gender Mainstreaming Action Groups (GMAGs) as well as incorporated this into the education curriculum.

The Prime Minister of Vietnam issued Decision 92/2001/QD-TTg setting out four tasks for the National Committee for the Advancement of Women (NCAW) which include working with various government agencies to carry out educational activities concerning the implementation of legislation and policy in relation to CEDAW and preparing national reports on the implementation of CEDAW. In Thailand, the Office of the Prime Minister has assigned the National Commission on Women's Affairs (ONCWA) to act as the focal point for promoting and coordinating women's affairs.[86] This has been transferred to the Ministry of Social

---

[86] Combined Fourth and Fifth Periodic Report: Thailand, CEDAW/C/THA/4–5, (24 June 2004) at para 23.

Development and Human Security as of 2002, under which the Office of Women's Affairs has been established.[87]

In Myanmar, the Ministry of Social Welfare, Relief and Resettlement is the designated focal ministry on gender related issues and has, in collaboration with various government agencies, UN bodies and NGOs, drawn up a National Plan of Action for the Advancement of Women (2011–15) addressing the twelve tasks set out by the Fourth World Conference on Women.[88] The Myanmar National Committee for Women's Affairs (MNCWA) was established in 1996 as a national mechanism for carrying out measures to promote the development of Myanmar women.[89] Women who wish to complain about gender-based discrimination can send letters of complaint to the Myanmar Women's Affairs Federation, formed on 20 December 2003 to implement the measures of the MNCWA.

In Lao PDR, the National Commission for the Advancement of Women (NCAW) was created by Prime Minister's Decree N.37/PM of 1 April 2003, tasked with developing comprehensive strategies to promote gender equality. The NCAW has prepared two national policy plans (2006–10; 2011–15)[90] for the advancement of women, pursuant to relevant

---

[87] Combined Fourth and Fifth Periodic Report: Thailand, CEDAW/C/THA/4-5, (24 June 2004) at para 24.

[88] Statement, Ms Aye Thidar Myo (Myanmar), Third Committee (Agenda Item 28), 66th UNGA, 12 October 2011, at: www.un.org/womenwatch/daw/documents/ga66/Myanmar.pdf.

[89] Initial Report to CEDAW Committee: Myanmar, CEDAW/C/MMR/1 at 8 (25 June 1999).

[90] www.unwomen-eseasia.org/docs/factsheets/04%20Lao%20PDR%20factsheet.pdf.

international treaties, the Beijing Platform of Action and Millennium Development Goals (MDGs). A further Order No.30/PM of 23 December 2004 instructs government bodies to set up committees on the advancement of women to implement policy and to report on this to the NCAW.[91]

In the Philippines, the National Commission on the Role of Filipino Women (NCRFW) was established on 7 January 1975 through Presidential Decree No. 633 to advise the President and the cabinet. It was renamed the Philippines Commission for Women, and its mandate was expanded by Republic Act 9710. It reviews and evaluates existing laws against CEDAW norms, recommends measures to ensure the integration of women in terms of socio-economic and cultural development at all levels, and monitors CEDAW state obligations and seeks to mainstream the application of its provisions. It seeks to get government agencies to use CEDAW-based gender indications and the Concluding Observations of the CEDAW Committee to promote the monitoring of the implementation of the Treaty.[92]

After acceding to CEDAW, the Malaysian government implemented a national plan of action (PoA) for the Advancement of Women in 1997.[93] In order to mainstream

[91] Combined Sixth and Seventh Periodic Report: Lao PDR, Part II: article 1 CEDAW/C/LAO/7 (30 May 2008) at 9–11.
[92] CEDAW in Southeast Asia: Philippines: http://cedaw-seasia.org/philippines_cedaw_implementation.html.
[93] Para 4, Statement, Hon Senator Norliza Abdul Rahim, Agenda Item 27 (Advancement of Women of the Third Committee), 67th Session, UNGA, 15 Oct 2012 at www.un.org/womenwatch/daw/documents/ga67/Malaysia.pdf.

gender perspectives into the development process, the government also reviewed legislation affecting women.

The Cabinet-level Ministry of Women, Family and Community Development (MWFCD) (*Kementerian Pembangunan Wanita, Keluarga dan Masyarakat* or KPWKM) was established in January 2001, headed by a female minister.[94] This was tasked with developing policies and goals aimed at achieving gender equality. This included undertaking research and developing programmes to ensure the incorporation of gender equality perspectives in the formation of general policies, such as the five-year 10th Malaysian Plan (2011–15)[95] policy formation. It adopted the specific policy target since 2004 of ensuring at least 30 per cent participation of women in decision-making positions within the public sector.[96] To aid focus on gender issues, senior officers in government ministries and agencies were appointed in 2005 as Gender Focal Points (GFP), as liasion

[94] This was originally called the Ministry of Women's Affairs on 17 January 2001 but its mandate was broadened to include family development, leading to a change of name on 15 February 2001. This was further broadened to include social welfare and development. Para 8, 'Responses to the list of issues and questions: Initial and Second Report: Malaysia', CEDAW/C/MYS/Q/2/Add.1 (27 March 2006).

[95] Para 9, Statement, Hon Senator Norliza Abdul Rahim, Agenda Item 27 (Advancement of Women of the Third Committee), 67th Session, UNGA, 15 Oct 2012 at www.un.org/womenwatch/daw/documents/ga67/Malaysia.pdf.

[96] Para 7, Statement, Hon Senator Norliza Abdul Rahim, Agenda Item 27 (Advancement of Women of the Third Committee), 67th Session, UNGA, 15 Oct 2012 at www.un.org/womenwatch/daw/documents/ga67/Malaysia.pdf.

officers for gender issues and to engage in information-gathering.[97]

The Malaysian Communications and Multimedia Content Code,[98] a set of industry guidelines, articulates the need to overcome 'biased portrayal on the basis of gender' within the context of promoting self-regulation. Breaches of these guidelines may be handled by the Complaints Bureau of the Communications and Multimedia Content Forum of Malaysia (CMCF), established in February 2001, under the auspices of the Communications and Multimedia Act 1998.

The Malaysian government also funds and supports the NAM Institute for the Empowerment of Women to show Malaysian experiences and best practices, particularly with 'fellow developing countries.'[99]

6.5 Promotional activities and non-legal approaches

To fulfill the CEDAW norm to eradicate gender stereotypes, ASEAN states have sought to promote this through law and policy. In Malaysia, the Ministry of Education

---

[97] Para 8, 'Responses to the list of issues and questions: Initial and Second Report: Malaysia', CEDAW/C/MYS/Q/2/Add.1 (27 March 2006).

[98] www.cmcf.my/onlineversion/part-1-introduction.

[99] Para 14, Statement, Hon Senator Norliza Abdul Rahim, Agenda Item 27 (Advancement of Women of the Third Committee), 67th Session, UNGA, 15 October 2012 at www.un.org/womenwatch/daw/documents/ga67/Malaysia.pdf.

169

issues guidelines to publishers or school textbooks which '[forbid] stereotyping of women as inferior to men' or as their 'followers or supporters rather than leaders or equal partners'.[100]

In an attempt to combat gender stereotypes and cultural patterns of conduct, the Cambodian government, in its Initial Report to the CEDAW committee, pointed out that under Article 36(3) of the Constitution '[t]he work by house-wives in the home shall have the same value as what they can receive when working outside the home.' This sought 'to promote behavioral change in men to recognize the role of women within the family, as well as in the society'.[101] Con-trary to Cambodian customs according to which parents match-make their daughters, Article 45 provides that mar-riage be 'based on the principle of mutual consent between one husband and one wife'.[102] This is reflected in Article 4 of the Law on Marriage and Family.

We close this section by drawing further attention to the use of non-legal approaches and its criticism. One of the primary criticisms levied by the CEDAW Committee against certain ASEAN states has been the lack of a legal solutions-oriented approach towards implementing CEDAW in the form of legally enforceable norms and monitoring

---

[100] Para 10, Para 8, 'Responses to the list of issues and questions: Initial and Second Report: Malaysia', CEDAW/C/MYS/Q/2/Add.1 (27 March 2006).

[101] Para 143, Combined Initial, Second and Third Periodic Reports of State Parties: Cambodia, CEDAW/C/KHM/1–3, (11 February 2004).

[102] Para 144, Combined Initial, Second and Third Periodic Reports of State Parties: Cambodia, CEDAW/C/KHM/1–3, (11 February 2004).

mechanisms. This may flow either from a preference to approach the issue through the more flexible vehicle of non-binding policy or from a fear of generating a complaints or rights-oriented culture focused on judicial solutions, as opposed to a petitionary one. There is, of course, a diversity of approaches within ASEAN states in this respect, as a facet of politico-legal culture, which is not static.

In relation to Vietnam, for example, the CEDAW Committee in 2001 was concerned about its 'lack of legal and other measures to address violence against women' and directed it to address a range of issues including 'high unemployment, polarization between rich and poor, social issues such as prostitution, as well as trafficking of women, drug abuse and sexually transmitted diseases'. It recommended that Vietnam 'monitor the implementation of legal provisions that guarantee women de jure equality'.[103]

Philippines, on the other hand, has a more robust rights culture insofar as individualised remedies are concerned. It acceded to the Optional Protocol to CEDAW[104] on 12 November 2003.[105] Article 2 of the

[103] Concluding Comments of the CEDAW Committee (CEDAW/C/2001/II/Add.8) at para 258.

[104] The Protocol was adopted by resolution A/RES/54/4 of 6 October 1999 at the fifty-fourth session of the General Assembly of the United Nations and entered into force on 22 December 2000: 2131 UNTS at 83.

[105] Cambodia (13 October 2010) and Thailand (14 June 2000) are also parties to the Optional Protocol to CEDAW; Indonesia signed it on 28 February 2000 but has not ratified it. Information available at: http://treaties.un.org/Pages/ViewDetails.aspx?src=TREATY&mtdsg_no=IV-8-b&chapter=4&lang=en.

Protocol[106] provides for a petition procedure by which individuals or groups of individuals under the jurisdiction of the state party claiming to be victims of specific violations of CEDAW norms have the standing to submit communications to the CEDAW committee. There is no provision for an *actio popularis* claiming systemic or abstract violations of CEDAW norms. Domestic remedies must first be exhausted unless the application of these would be 'unreasonably prolonged or unlikely to bring effective relief.'[107] The Committee is obliged to transmits its views on the communication to the parties concerned (Article 7). State parties are at only subject to the weak obligation to 'give due consideration' to Committee views and recommendations, and shall submit a written response within 6 months of any action taken, it must also 'facilitate access to information' of Committee views and recommendations on matters involving that state party (Article 13). In the case of *Karen Tayag Vertido v The Philippines*,[108] the CEDAW Committee found that the acquittal of a rape case by the Philippines Supreme Court violated

---

[106] 'Communications may be submitted by or on behalf of individuals or groups of individuals, under the jurisdiction of a State Party, claiming to be victims of a violation of any of the rights set forth in the Convention by that State Party. Where a communication is submitted on behalf of individuals or groups of individuals, this shall be with their consent unless the author can justify acting on their behalf without such consent.'

[107] Article 4, Optional Protocol CEDAW.

[108] CEDAW Committee, Communication No. 18/2008, CEDAW/C/46/D/18/2008 (1 September 2008).

Articles 2(f)[109] and 5(a) of CEDAW, given the evidence indicating wrongful gender stereotyping in that the judge was influenced by her vision of what the 'rational and ideal response of a woman in a rape situation'[110] should be. The Committee recommended that the author of the communication be provided 'appropriate compensation commensurate with the gravity of the violations of her rights' and also asked that Congress review rape legislation; in an attempt to address systemic gender discrimination, it recommended that gender-sensitive training be provided for judges, lawyers and other law enforcement and medical personnel, to avoid the revictimisation of women who report that they were raped.[111]

---

[109] Article 2(f) CEDAW: 'To take all appropriate measures, including legislation, to modify or abolish existing laws, regulations, customs and practices which constitute discrimination against women.'

[110] CEDAW Committee, Communication No. 18/2008, CEDAW/C/46/D/18/2008 (1 Sept 2008), para 8.5.

[111] CEDAW Committee, Communication No. 18/2008, CEDAW/C/46/D/18/2008 (1 Sept 2008), para 8.9.

Chapter 7

Joint ASEAN agreements

While the ASEAN Secretary-General (ASG) has entered into agreements, especially Memoranda of Understanding (MOUs), either on behalf of ASEAN as an IO or, in exceptional cases, on behalf of the governments of ASEAN where so authorised, the ASG has so far made limited use of the potentially more encompassing competences in the conduct of external relations. It seems yet a distant practice that ASEAN as an IO would enter into international agreements, which would then create hard obligations for the Member States. The agreements that matter are concluded as plurilateral agreements (Chapter 5). But many of such, on the surface, plurilateral agreements, may also be considered slightly differently as joint ASEAN agreements. The parties to these agreements are still states, but the fact that the states on one side of the agreement, in one column of the signatures, together form ASEAN is not without effect. From a strictly formalist point of view, the difference between plurilateral and joint ASEAN agreements is indeed slim, almost non-existent. What we are proposing is a different reading. And the way in which they are read, we submit, does make a difference. What is more, a different reading of plurilateral agreements as joint ASEAN agreements is not only possible, but also warranted so as to credit the principle of ASEAN centrality.

In this chapter, we set out the argument that many of ASEAN's external relations, in critical fields such as economic relations, may well be understood as a form of joint ASEAN agreements. In particular, while rights and obligations rest with Member States, the role of the Secretariat is enhanced, and external agreements can show an internal effect in the relationship between ASEAN as a distinct entity and its Member States. What is more, we suggest that there is a strong argument in favour of harmonious interpretation by members, not only of the Charter and internal agreements, but of external agreements as well.

Specifically, by involving ASEAN in external agreements, Member States' commitments in such agreements might be subject to monitoring and review within the framework of ASEAN in a way that can be (but need not be) connected to the enforcement mechanisms of the external agreement itself. These are internal effects of the ASEAN legal regime.[1] The main anchor for this line of argument rests in obligations of membership. We thus pick up argumentative threads of the previous section. Overall, the present section supports the contention that 'external legal obligations embedded in the external agreements ... indirectly and perhaps inadvertently lead to a greater internal integration'.[2]

But what role would there be for ASEAN to play in external relations if – as the previous section argued – it itself

---

[1] See Section 2.5 on the notion of ASEAN legal regime as opposed to ASEAN legal order.

[2] Cremona, Venesson and Lee, 'The External Agreements of ASEAN', at 7. Cf B. Reinalda, 'ASEAN as an Informal Organization: Does it Exist and Does it Have Agency? The Emergence of the ASEAN Secretariat', in J. E. Oestreich (ed.), *International Organizations as Self-Directed Actors* (Abingdon, Oxon: Routledge 2012) at 236.

does not incur significant binding commitments, let alone impose obligations on its Member States? We suggest that it has a role to play in *channeling information, facilitating compliance, monitoring,* and *dispute settlement* in relation to ASEAN external agreements. The functions ASEAN can perform in this regard are conferred to it under the Charter as well as under external agreements, even if Member States are the primary addressees of ASEAN external agreements.

The prima facie evidence for such a view stems from the ways in which external agreements treat ASEAN Member States: that is differently from state parties in plurilateral international agreements that are unconnected to the membership of any IO. For example, Article 78 of the 2008 Economic Partnership Agreement with Japan provides that '[f]or the ASEAN Member States, this Agreement including its amendments shall be deposited with the Secretary-General of ASEAN, who shall promptly furnish a certified copy thereof, to each ASEAN Member State'.[3] This may be mere symbolism, or, as we argue in this section, part of joint ASEAN agreements. That agreement and others contain more specific consequences connected to the fact that a group of Member States collectively forms ASEAN when it comes to a treaty's termination. Article 80(2) of the agreement with Japan states that '[t]his Agreement shall terminate either when all ASEAN Member States which are Parties withdraw ... or when Japan does so.' Article 24 of the Economic Cooperation Agreement with India specifies that

[3] Agreement on Comprehensive Economic Partnership among Japan and Member States of the Association of Southeast Asian Nations (2008).

termination must be by written notice, whether from India or 'ASEAN Member States collectively'.[4]

Difference might also arise if joint ASEAN agreements are breached. If an ASEAN Member State were to breach obligations of external agreements which does not detail dispute settlement mechanisms, it might be argued, that the default mechanism of the law of treaties – suspension of treaty obligations according to Article 60 VCLT – would not apply in relation to other ASEAN Member States. Rather, breaches would be treated as instances of non-compliance.[5] It is still unclear what those consequences are, as is the nature of the dispute settlement procedures of ASEAN.

This section first distinguishes joint ASEAN agreements from what is known in the context of European legal integration as mixed agreements (1). It then gives further shape to what we term joint ASEAN agreements and justifies this type of external agreements as distinct from plurilateral agreements. We highlight the principle of ASEAN centrality and discuss the scope of obligations of membership (2). This discussion has implications for how institutions of Member

---

[4] Agreement on Trade in Goods under the Framework Agreement on Comprehensive Economic Cooperation between the Republic of India and the Association of Southeast Asian Nations, Bangkok, Thailand, 13 August 2009.

[5] Compare J. Klabbers, 'Compliance Procedures', in D. Bodansky, J. Brunnée and E. Hey (eds.), *The Oxford Handbook of International Environmental Law* (Oxford: Oxford University Press, 2007) 995 at 1002; M. Koskenniemi, 'Breach of Treaty or Non-Compliance? Reflections on the Enforcement of the Montreal Protocol' (1992) 3 *Yearbook of International Environmental Law* 123–162.

States deal with joint ASEAN external agreements (3) and for the way the roles of the Secretariat are perceived (4). We highlight specifically the notable role given to the Secretariat in interpreting the Charter and the interaction of the Secretariat with other ASEAN institutions in matters of dispute settlement (5).

7.1 An (ill-)fitting comparison: mixed agreements

It has been common in the external relations of the European Community that both the Community and its Member States are contracting parties, specifically in cases where external agreements involve areas of competence of the Community as well as of the Member States, or where competence is shared.[6] This practice is basically a mechanism for dealing with external agreements for the conclusion of which neither the Union nor the Member States have *exclusive* competence. This is the typical scenario: the WTO agreement was, for example, concluded as a mixed agreement on the part of the European Community (EC) and its Member States at that time because certain modes of supplying services under the GATS and parts of the TRIPS

---

[6] On the appeal of mixity as an expression of true federalism, see J. H. H. Weiler, 'The External Legal Relations of Non-Unitary Actors: Mixity and the Federal Principle', in J. H. H. Weiler, *The Constitution of Europe* (Cambridge: Cambridge University Press, 1999) 130–187; P. J. Kuijper, 'Of "Mixity" and "Double-hatting"' Inaugural Lecture (Vossiuspers UvA 2008).

Agreement did not fall under the EC's exclusive competence in matters of common commercial policy.[7]

The practice of mixed agreements has given rise to a number of legal and policy questions, including issues regarding the later evolution of competence, possible uncertainty on the part of third parties' liability, and the decision on who negotiates.[8] The root cause of these issues lies in the internal division of competences between the European Union and its Member States.

In many instances, mixed agreements could actually have been avoided, if the Council had only been willing to more readily recognize the exclusive competences of the Community.[9] But, as Claus-Dieter Ehlermann noted, 'Member States wished to continue to appear as contracting parties in order to remain visible and identifiable actors on the international scene.'[10] The Commission often times preferred not to pick a fight and consented to the practice of 'mixity'.

ASEAN Member States remain largely adamant about the fact that they do not want to compromise their sovereignty by conferring competences onto ASEAN as an IO. Certainly, they wish to retain their strong say in international relations. Any involvement of ASEAN in

---

[7] Opinion 1/94 of 15 November 1994, [1994] ECR I-5267.

[8] E. Paasivirta and P. J. Kuijper, 'Does One Size Fit All?: The European Community and the Responsibility of International Organizations' (2005) 36 *Netherlands Yearbook of International Law* 169–226.

[9] See C.-D. Ehlermann, 'Mixed Agreements – A List of Problems', in Keeffe and Schermers (eds.) *Mixed Agreements* (Leiden: Kluwer, 1983) 6.

[10] *Ibid.*

external relations would in fact not be due to a division of competence at all, as competence rests solely with Member States. Whereas mixity in the European context grew out of internal divisions of competence and internal decision-making, ASEAN's involvement in external relations is not the result of such a division of competence. Any close analogy between what we call joint ASEAN agreements and mixed agreements would therefore risk being misleading.

The fact that ASEAN as a collective *and* its Member States are involved has quite different reasons and a different trajectory. Oftentimes ASEAN is engaged in external relations not because of conferred competences and express authorisation by virtue of its Charter, but because Member States grant it a role in their external agreements. Through external agreements, it seems, ASEAN gains authority in relation to its members. In addition, the fact that one side of the external agreements collectively forms ASEAN has repercussions for the institutions of Member States. We will deal with these two levels of internal effects of joint ASEAN external agreements – for Members and for ASEAN as a distinct entity – in turn. They both build on the principle of ASEAN centrality and on the scope of obligations of membership.

7.2 ASEAN centrality and obligations of membership

What role does ASEAN, specifically its Secretariat, play under the Charter in relation to external agreements? Moreover, do obligations arise from ASEAN membership regarding compliance with external agreements? In this sub-section we focus on the roles that organs of ASEAN as an IO play in joint ASEAN agreements. Those agreements have ASEAN Member States as their parties and, notably, we do not suggest that ASEAN implements or enforces treaty commitments that it might have as an IO in relation to Member States. We thus read the ASEAN Charter again closely to support the view that the ASEAN Secretariat has a role to play with regard to external agreements between Member States and other parties.

First, among the purposes of ASEAN, Article 1 lists 'maintain[ing] the centrality and proactive role of ASEAN as the primary driving force in its relations and cooperation with its external partners in a regional architecture that is open, transparent and inclusive'. In pursuit of its purposes, Article 2 continues, ASEAN and its Member States shall adhere to principles that include 'enhanced consultations on matters seriously affecting the common interest of ASEAN' (lit. g), 'upholding ... international law' (lit. j), and 'adherence to multilateral trade rules and ASEAN's rules-based regimes for effective implementation of economic commitments and progressive reduction towards elimination of all barriers to regional economic integration' (lit. n).

The notion of 'ASEAN centrality' is significant. It is expressed not only in Article 1, but also in the Economic Community Blueprint (para 65) and in a number of other instruments. Article 41(3) of the Charter reaffirms: 'ASEAN shall be the primary driving force in regional arrangements that it initiates and maintain its centrality in regional cooperation and community building.' The idea of ASEAN centrality is primarily directed at the coordinated conduct of external relations. But if ASEAN is supposed to take a 'pro-active role . . . as the primary driving force' in its external relations, then it seems plausible to extend this approach to fostering its role in the internal implementation of external agreements.

In support of such a role, it might then be suggested that Member States are obligated to cooperate with the ASEAN Secretariat to this effect as part of their obligations of membership. Article 5 of the Charter provides the anchor of our inquiry in this regard. It provides that:

> 2. Member States shall take all necessary measures, including the enactment of appropriate domestic legislation, to effectively implement the provisions of this Charter and to comply with all obligations of membership.

> 3. In the case of a serious breach of the Charter or noncompliance, the matter shall be referred to Article 20.

As part of general international law, Member States are obliged not to frustrate the functioning of ASEAN as an IO in the realization of its principles and objectives; that may reasonably be seen as implied in Article 5 of the Charter.[11] It might also be based in a general principle of good faith, which is a universally recognised principle according to the Vienna Convention on the Law of Treaties between States and

---

[11] For a comparative assessment of such clauses on the obligations of membership see H. G. Schermers and N. Blokker, *International Institutional Law*, 5th edn. (Leiden: Martinus Nijhoff, 2011) 19–20.

International Organizations or between International Organizations.[12]
The scope and reach of the obligations of membership depends significantly on how the Charter is interpreted and construed. Notably then, the ASEAN Secretariat has an opportunity to play an active role in this regard. Article 51 ASEAN Charter provides that:

> Upon the request of any Member State, *the interpretation of the Charter shall be undertaken by the ASEAN Secretariat* in accordance with the rules of procedure determined by the ASEAN Coordinating Council.

If the ASEAN Secretary-General plays his or her cards well, it might well be that the Secretariat builds up interpretative authority over time and thereby influences the development of the Charter generally. It could specifically impact the development of obligations of membership and, with regard to external relations, contribute to shaping answers to the question of how Member States' commitments under joint ASEAN external agreements are connected to such obligations of membership.

Furthermore, and most importantly, if compliance with ASEAN external agreements qualifies as an obligation of membership, disputes concerning compliance are subject to dispute settlement mechanisms under the Charter and subject to other *internal* agreements that further specify how

---

[12] Preamble, Vienna Convention on the Law of Treaties between States and International Organizations or between International Organizations, 21 March 1986.

to deal with disputes pertaining to internal obligations. Obligations of membership could thus potentially internalise reactions to breaches of external agreements. Such internal mechanisms could run in parallel or even in exclusion of dispute settlement mechanisms that the external agreements themselves might foresee. Internal and external agreements may well differ with regard to their dispute settlement mechanisms, specifically as to *who* can initiate proceedings, *when*, and under *what* conditions. To be clear, we suggest that those internal mechanisms in parallel or to the exclusion of other mechanisms operate with regard to the relations between Member States, not in relation to any ASEAN member and third parties to an external agreement.

Whether such kind of internalisation of disputes about ASEAN external agreements by virtue of obligations of membership is plausible also depends on the interpretation of Article 24 of the Charter, which provides that '[d]isputes relating to specific ASEAN instruments shall be settled through the mechanisms and procedures provided for in such instruments.' This could be read so as to speak against potentially treating breaches of external agreements as conflicting with obligations of membership. At the same time, it could just as well be read not to preclude that compliance measures in such cases are taken because conflicts with obligations of membership are a matter of the Charter.

We continue by highlighting the implications of the principle of ASEAN centrality and a wide reading of obligations of membership to include compliance with joint external agreements for both the institutions of ASEAN Member States and of ASEAN as a distinct entity. The two are linked in the sense that increasing harmony in the ways in which ASEAN Member States deal with external agreements might mitigate the need for greater monitoring and possibly compliance by ASEAN. In turn, central oversight might induce further harmonisation.

7.3 Consequences for member state institutions: ASEAN centrality

What are the consequences that arise for Member States from a characterisation of external agreements as joint ASEAN agreements? Those consequences will continue to depend on some extent on members' constitutional arrangements, as we described in Chapters 5 and 6. It is precisely those differences that further add to the importance of involving ASEAN in one way or another, such as in supervisory, implementing and monitoring functions.

Apart from the question of how those functions of the Secretariat or possibly of the Summit are received within Member States, we focus on *what difference it might make domestically that external agreements are joint ASEAN agreements rather than any other international agreement.* In our analysis, we again place emphasis on the notion of ASEAN centrality. If ASEAN centrality takes hold as a cultural anchor, domestic practices might further support indirect effects such as 'harmonious interpretation' that go beyond those already discussed in Chapter 5.

In this context then it might be worth recalling how strong Article 5(2) of the Charter is phrased. It obliges Member States to:

> take *all necessary measures*, including the enactment of appropriate domestic legislation, to effectively implement the provisions of this Charter and to *comply with all obligations of membership*.

It is understandable that legislation is singled out as one such measure to implement the Charter and to comply with obligations of membership given the largely 'dualist' constitutional structure of most ASEAN Member States. Domestic administrations and courts are by default not in a position to apply the Charter or ASEAN external agreements directly.

That said, understanding external agreements as collectively ASEAN agreements points to duties of cooperation towards other ASEAN Member States and towards ASEAN as an IO specifically towards its Secretariat and its Summit. But beyond that, it requires 'harmonious interpretation'. This principle specifically speaks to administrations and the judiciary. Such a demand would by no means be far-fetched if complying with ASEAN external agreements were an obligation of membership, as we have discussed above.[13] But even without this link between external and internal obligations, ASEAN centrality could affect how domestic institutions treat ASEAN external agreements.

The documented practice of some ASEAN Member States of giving indirect effect to international law that we have discussed in Chapter 4 would thus apply *a fortiori* to joint ASEAN agreements. There should arguably be a yet

---

[13] Section 6.2.

more forceful presumption that domestic legal instruments are consistent with joint ASEAN agreements.[14]

For the time being, no institution within ASEAN would make a claim that ASEAN instruments have direct effect within Member States.[15] At the same time, ASEAN instruments can have indirect effects in the sense that domestic law must be interpreted in their light, wherever possible. That would support the functioning of ASEAN. The argument here runs parallel to what we said about indirect effect in our discussion of plurilateral agreements.[16] If anything, such effects might be deemed to be yet stronger because they would give effect to the obligations of membership. In particular domestic courts might be willing and in a position to possibly hold executives to their ASEAN commitments and to safeguard compliance.[17]

As of now, as the discussion of plurilateral agreements has also shown, the practice of ASEAN Member States diverges when it comes to their treatment of international

---

[14] See Section 6.2. See also *The Sahand* [2011] 2 SLR 1093, Singaporean case following UK case: *ex p Brind* [1991] 1 AC 696.

[15] That remains a feature largely confined to European Law. See, in detail on the fate of supremacy and direct effect in the Andean Community, K. J. Alter, L. R. Helfer and O. Saldías, 'Transplanting the European Court of Justice: The Experience of the Andean Tribunal of Justice' (2012) 60 *American Journal of Comparative Law* 629–664 (summarizing that the Andean Tribunal of Justice 'declined to transform the Cartagena Agreement into a constitution for the Andean Community, it refused to imply powers for Andean authorities, and it refrained from requiring national judges to give effect to its rulings')

[16] Section 3.2.

[17] Desierto, 'ASEAN's Constitutionalization of International Law', 313.

law. Oftentimes it is unsettled and remain in a state of flux. Against this backdrop, the functions of the Secretariat and dispute settlement processes are of increased importance as they can potentially work towards greater harmony between Member State institutions.[18]

7.4 Functions of the Secretariat

The functions that the ASEAN Secretariat could be envisaged to perform in relation to external agreements might resemble those of non-compliance mechanisms.[19] It is those mechanisms that are within reach, rather than infringement procedures such as those within the context of the European Union where the Commission can act on its own initiative to investigate Member States' measures and can even impose heavy sanctions. In contrast, the ASEAN Secretariat may perform governance functions and aim at compliance through mechanisms such as channeling information, facilitating compliance, monitoring and, when it comes to it, dispute settlement.

Such modes of governance have, on occasion, proved to be no less significant instances of public authority than the exercise of 'hard' powers such as imposing fines or penalties. In the absence of mechanisms of coercion, the authority of the

---

[18] *Ibid.* 303–304.

[19] R. Churchill and G. Ulfstein, 'Autonomous Institutional Arrangements in Multilateral Environmental Arrangements: A Little-Noticed Phenomenon in International Law' (2000) 94 *American Journal of International Law* 623–659; Koskenniemi, 'Breach of Treaty'.

actor is, however, of crucial importance. Factors that matter greatly under these circumstances include, for instance, the prestige of the Secretary-General as well as a stock of expertise and, in this sense, 'epistemic authority'.[20] Finally, it is again interesting to note that the Secretariat's functions may in fact grow through provisions in external agreements.

7.4.1 Channeling information, coordination

Treaties like the TAC[21] tend to contain vague obligations, such as to collaborate for the acceleration of regional growth, to intensify economic cooperation through adopting appropriate regional strategies for economic development and mutual assistance.[22] Other economic agreements may be more specific in identifying areas of cooperation. The agreement between ASEAN and Russia specifies for example that cooperation should extend to '[small and medium sized enterprises], science and technology, energy, mineral resource utilization, transport, IT and communication technology, HR development cooperation, environmental management and

---

[20] Further research along these lines might well draw inspiration from the role of secretariats in environmental regimes. See S. Bauer, 'Does Bureaucracy Really Matter? The Authority of Intergovernmental Treaty Secretariats in Global Environmental Politics' (2006) 6 *Global Environmental Politics* 24–49; see also I. Venzke, 'International Bureaucracies in a Political Science Perspective – Agency, Authority and International Institutional Law' (2008) 9 *German Law Journal* 1401–1428.

[21] Treaty of Amity and Cooperation in Southeast Asia, Bali, Indonesia, 24 February 1976.

[22] Arts. 6–7 TAC.

protection, tourism, sports and culture'.[23] Obligations
between ASEAN states and third parties may be to ensure
effective protection of intellectual property rights obtained as
a result of cooperation or prohibition from disclosing confidential information.[24] Notably, such treaties may not enter
into force until the ASEAN Secretary-General is informed
that the Parties 'have completed their internal procedures'
necessary for its entry into force.[25] Such cooperative treaties
merely identify areas for cooperation without specification of
how to go about this endeavor.[26] The Secretariat might
assume such tasks. It is already explicitly asked to do so in a
number of MOUs.

The 2009 Memorandum of Understanding between
ASEAN and the People's Republic of China (PRC) on
Strengthening Cooperation in the Field of Standards, Technical Regulations and Conformity Assessment explicitly refers
to the coordinating role of the ASEAN Secretariat. Article 3

---

[23] Agreement between the Governments of the Member Countries of the
ASEAN and the Government of the Russian Federation on Economic
and Development Cooperation 2005.

[24] Arts. 4, 8, Agreement between the Governments of the Member
Countries of the ASEAN and the Government of the Russian Federation
on Economic and Development Cooperation 2005.

[25] Art. 11, Agreement on Trade in Goods under the Framework Agreement
on Comprehensive Economic Cooperation between the ASEAN and the
Republic of India 2009.

[26] Agreement on Cultural Cooperation between the Governments of the
Member States of the ASEAN and the Government of the Russian
Federation 2010 (cooperation on training of skills in culture and art, to
prevent illegal export and import of cultural property, conserving
museums, facilitating contacts in the field of folk culture etc. . .).

provides that 'ASEAN Member States shall designate their respective competent authorities to be responsible for the implementation of this Memorandum of Understanding and designate the ASEAN Secretariat as the coordinating body for ASEAN.'[27] The ASEAN Secretariat has also been the executing agency, together with the third party state, that is tasked with implementing MOUs such as that with the Ministry of Agriculture of the PRC on Agricultural Cooperation. The MOU provides that project formulation, implementation and monitoring should be carried out 'through existing ASEAN-China Agricultural Committees or bilateral discussions', absent any liaison bodies.[28]

A MOU may furthermore set out a commitment to develop practical strategies in identified fields, undertake to support joint research, facilitate cooperation between government agencies, commit to regular meetings and allocate financial responsibilities and stipulate a procedure for suspension. MOUs between ASEAN as an IO and other IOs may also provide for exchanging information on best practices on issues of mutual interests.[29] This mode of external agreement, more closely linked to the first type that we described in Chapter 4, interacts with joint ASEAN agreements.

---

[27] See also Article III (1) 'The Ministry of Communications of the People's Republic of China and the ASEAN Secretariat shall be the agencies responsible for the identification, coordination, implementation and monitoring of projects and activities conducted pursuant to this Memorandum of Understanding.' Art III(2) of the MOU between ASEAN and PRC on Transport Cooperation 2004.

[28] Art III (Implementation).

[29] Article II, MOU between the ASEAN Secretariat and SCO Secretariat.

Lastly, other ASEAN agreements confer functions on the ASG relating to publicity as well as to the provision and dissemination of information. For example, paragraph 7 of the ASEAN Intergovernmental Commission on Human Rights (AICHR) Terms of Reference (TOR) stipulates the functions of the Secretary-General and ASEAN Secretariat, which include bringing relevant issues to the attention of AICHR and concurrently informing the ASEAN Foreign Ministers.

7.4.2 *Implementation and facilitating compliance*

With regard to joint ASEAN agreements, the Secretariat may further perform functions relating to the implementation of agreements in a way that facilitates compliance.[30] The Operational Certification Procedures, that form part of the ASEAN-Australia-New Zealand FTA (AANZFTA) and aim at implementing rules of origin, for example, provide that:

> The Certificate of Origin shall be issued by an Issuing Authority/Body of the exporting Party. Details of the Issuing Authorities/Bodies shall be notified by each Party, through the ASEAN Secretariat, prior to the entry into force of this Agreement. Any subsequent changes shall be promptly notified by each Party, through the ASEAN Secretariat.

Other agreements open up opportunities for the Secretariat, too. The 2008 Economic Partnership Agreement with Japan,

---

[30] See generally Klabbers, 'Compliance Procedures'.

for example, stipulates in Article 47 that '[e]ach Party shall designate an enquiry point which shall have the responsibility to coordinate the implementation of this Chapter.' The Chapter at issue concerns 'Standards, Technical Regulations and Conformity Assessment Procedures'. It would in principle be conceivable that the ASEAN Secretariat acted as an enquiry point.

7.4.3 Monitoring

According to Article 11(2)(b) of the Charter, the ASG shall 'facilitate and monitor progress in the implementation of ASEAN agreements and decisions, and submit an annual report on the work of ASEAN to the ASEAN Summit'. The provision does not specify what is meant by ASEAN agreements. In particular, it does not say whether those are only internal agreements or whether they include external agreements just as well. Paragraph (d) provides further that the ASG shall 'present the views of ASEAN and participate in meetings with external parties in accordance with approved policy guidelines and mandate given to the Secretary-General'. This at least indicates that Article 11 and the functions of the ASG are by no means confined to the internal setting. The ASG's practice of signing external agreements also bears this out.

In addition, the Secretariat maintains a list summarising the status of ASEAN internal and external agreements. The ASEAN Secretariat Resource Center (ARC) is responsible for the process of certifying ASEAN Agreements and the dissemination of the certified true copies to all ASEAN

Member States and other parties as required.[31] This existing practice could be read so as to support the view that the ASEAN Secretariat does have a role also in monitoring external agreements.

Many external agreements actually require the establishment of some sort of joint body or the appointment of coordinating agencies to implement the agreement. Article 15 of the 1993 Agreement between ASEAN and the Government of Canada on Economic Cooperation, for example, provides that Contracting Parties 'agree to establish a Joint Cooperation Committee (JCC) to promote and review the various cooperation activities envisaged between the member countries of ASEAN and Canada under this Agreement'. In addition, consultations may be the vehicle through which the Parties decide the specifics in terms of implementing the cooperation an MOU calls for.[32]

Other agreements relate to designating coordinating agencies to promote cooperation in relation to terrorism,[33] non-traditional security issues (drug and people trafficking,

---

[31] ASEAN Secretariat Resource Center, www.asean.org/asean/asean-secretariat/asean-secretariat-resource-centre-arc.

[32] Art III(2) of the MOU between ASEAN and PRC in Non-Traditional Security Issues 2004 – 'The implementing agencies of the Parties shall determine *through consultation* the details, schedule and arrangements *for the implementation of the cooperation* provided in this Memorandum of Understanding, and *shall serve as coordinators for such cooperation*.'

[33] Para 9 of the ASEAN-Canada Joint Declaration for Cooperation to Combat International Terrorism 2006 ('designate a contact point to coordinate their respective law enforcement and security agencies, authorities dealing with countering terrorist financing and other relevant agencies *for the purposes of implementing the declaration*').

money laundering, international economic crime and cyber crime),[34] or transport.[35] Some agreements provide for 'regular' consultation mechanisms[36] while others are more specific and call for annual meetings in specific countries.[37] Still others call for a body, which will oversee and review implementation of an agreement.[38] All these efforts of monitoring and implementation open up opportunities for the ASEAN Secretariat as well.

7.5 Dispute settlement mechanisms

The Secretariat interacts with other institutions when it comes to issues of dispute settlement. One of the Secretariat's

[34] Art III(2) of the MOU between ASEAN and PRC in Non-Traditional Security Issues 2004.

[35] Art III(2) of the MOU between ASEAN and PRC on Transport Cooperation 2004 ('The identification, implementation, monitoring and appraisal of the joint cooperation projects and activities shall be undertaken through the ASEAN-China Senior Transport Officials Meeting, for final consideration and approval by the ASEAN-China Transport Ministers Meeting').

[36] Art 3 of the MOU between ASEAN and PRC on Strengthening Cooperation in the Field of Standards, TRs and Conformity Assessment.

[37] Art IV of the MOU between ASEAN and PRC on Maritime Consultation Mechanism 2010 – 'Aiming at a close cooperation in the *effective implementation* of this Memorandum of Understanding, meetings of the *ASEAN-China Maritime Consultation Mechanism* will be convened once a year in China.'

[38] Art. 14 of the Agreement on Trade in Goods under the Framework Agreement on Comprehensive Economic Cooperation among ASEAN and ROK 2006 – 'The institutions as provided for in Article 5.3 of the Framework Agreement *shall oversee, supervise, coordinate and review, as appropriate, the implementation of this Agreement.*'

functions that is of key relevance here is its interpretation of the Charter, and thus also its take on the primary question of whether compliance with joint ASEAN external agreements qualifies as an obligation of membership. The rules of procedure for requesting the ASEAN Secretariat to interpret the ASEAN Charter have now been adopted in Phnom Penh on 2 April 2012 by the ASEAN Coordinating Council.[39]

Any member may request that the Secretariat interpret the Charter, mentioning the article(s) at issue and the specific interpretative questions pertaining to it. The Secretariat invites all other members to express their views within sixty days.[40] After that the Secretariat has thirty days to render its interpretation.[41] The procedure is thus not only characterized by a remarkably strict time frame, but also invests the Secretariat with a notable degree of autonomy. Even if the Secretariat may well seek an accommodating interpretation that finds the consensus of most, if not all, members, and even if it renders its interpretation in consultation with interested members, it ultimately has the authority to decide on the interpretation of the Charter, without this decision being formally subject to further control by the members. Moreover, the rules state that the Secretariat's interpretations shall be reasoned, which further allows for the setting out of a vision of ASEAN.[42]

With regard to dispute settlement more generally, the Charter itself provides one mechanism in Article 20 (4) which

---

[39] See 2012 Rules of Procedure for the Interpretation of The ASEAN Charter, available at http://cil.nus.edu.sg.
[40] Rule 4(3).   [41] Rule 4(4).   [42] Rule 5(b).

states that '[i]n case of a serious breach of the Charter or non-compliance, the matter shall be referred to the ASEAN Summit for decision.' According to Article 7 ASEAN Charter, the ASEAN Summit 'shall comprise the Heads of State or Government of the Member States'. It shall 'be the supreme policy-making body of ASEAN', and shall:

> deliberate, provide policy guidance and take decisions on key issues pertaining to the realization of the objectives of ASEAN, important matters of interest to Member States and all issues referred to it by the ASEAN Coordinating Council, the ASEAN Community Councils and ASEAN Sectoral Ministerial Bodies

The text of this provision leaves a lot of room for interpretation. If ASEAN centrality is indeed a key objective next to all the other principles that would support a role of ASEAN in external relations, the Summit could also be involved in ensuring Member States' compliance with external agreements.

The Summit shall further 'decide on matters referred to it under Chapters VII and VIII'.[43] Those two chapters deal with decision-making and settlement of disputes and thus take up the role of the Summit in matters of serious breaches and non-compliance.[44] The role of the Summit when it comes to compliance with ASEAN joint agreements remains open to some speculation. But it seems as though a Member State could well bring the non-compliance of one member onto the agenda so as to seek internal compliance with external agreements.

[43] Art. 7(2) ASEAN Charter.   [44] Art. 20(4) ASEAN Charter.

Two issues are specifically noteworthy. First, Article 20 mentions both 'serious breach' and 'non-compliance' as triggers for a matter to be referred to the Summit. These two thresholds traditionally belong to two different sets of situations: *serious breach* is the language of treaty obligations (Article 60 VCLT); *non-compliance* is the language of multilateral treaties that set up institutional mechanisms.[45] Second, the formulation of Article 20 in passive voice gives no indication as to *who* can refer a matter to the Summit. Presumably Member States can do so. But can any Member State do so or would it have to show injury or a further qualified interest? It is furthermore questionable whether the ASEAN Secretariat might also refer a matter to the Summit. These, again, are matters of interpretation to which the Secretariat itself might add its voice.

Furthermore, the ASEAN Secretary-General may in his *ex officio* capacity provide 'good offices, conciliation or mediation' upon request of parties to a dispute.[46] According to the Protocol to the ASEAN Charter on Dispute Settlement Mechanism (2010), the Secretariat furthermore administers the ASEAN Dispute Settlement Mechanism Fund, which is

---

[45] Koskenniemi, 'Breach of Treaty'.

[46] Art 23, ASEAN Charter. Art 6, Protocol to the ASEAN Charter (2010). Financing Memorandum between the European Community and Government of Brunei Darussalam for the ASEAN-EC Management Centre 1994. The Preamble reads that the Commission of the European Communities is 'acting for and on behalf of the European Community' while Brunei as host country was 'acting for and on behalf of the Association of South-East Asian Nations and referred to as "the recipient" or "the beneficiary countries"'.

separate from its regular budget. Funded by parties to the dispute, the ASEAN Secretariat under Article 18 of the Protocol bears the:

> responsibility of assisting the arbitral tribunals and persons providing good offices, mediation and conciliation, especially on the legal, historical and the procedural aspects of the matters dealt with, and of providing secretarial and technical support.

The Secretariat provides similar assistance to the Panels and Appellate Body under Article 19. It also receives all dispute-related documentation, and it assists in the monitoring of the implementation of the findings and recommendations of the Appellate Body.[47]

The Protocol is administered by the Senior Economic Officials Meeting (SEOM) which may establish a panel charged with making an 'objective assessment' of a dispute before it in confidential proceedings.[48] Interested third party Member States with a substantial interest in a matter will have the rights and obligations of a Third Party after due notification is made.[49] They are entitled to be heard[50] and to receive the Parties' submission to the first substantive meeting of the arbitral tribunal.[51]

---

[47] See in further detail G. J. Naldi, 'The ASEAN Protocol on Dispute Settlement Mechanisms: An Appraisal' (2014) 5 *Journal of International Dispute Settlement* 105–138.

[48] Arts. 7 and 8, ASEAN Protocol on Enhanced Dispute Settlement Mechanism (2004).

[49] Art. 13(1), Protocol to the ASEAN Charter (2010).

[50] Art. 13(2), Protocol to the ASEAN Charter (2010).

[51] Art. 13(3), Protocol to the ASEAN Charter (2010).

Their submissions will also be given to the parties to the dispute.[52]

Decisions of the Panel are subject to appellate review[53] by a body established by the ASEAN Economic Ministers. The Panel or Appellate Body is empowered to recommend that the concerned Member State take action, where a measure is inconsistent with an agreement, to ensure conformity with it.[54] The SEOM shall 'keep under surveillance'[55] the implementation of the recommendations, which must be complied with within sixty days of their adoption, unless there is a request for a longer period of time, which 'shall not be unreasonably denied' (e.g. need to pass national legislation).[56] It is to have the assistance of the ASEAN Secretariat in monitoring the implementation, including its support for the collection and transmission of the relevant documentation.[57] This fairly elaborate, rule-oriented procedure distances dispute settlement from bureaucratic means and downplays consensus-seeking as the modus operandi.[58] This also has the potential of strengthening the Secretariat.

---

[52] Art. 13(2), Protocol to the ASEAN Charter (2010).

[53] Art. 12, ASEAN Protocol on Enhanced Dispute Settlement Mechanism (2004).

[54] Art. 14, ASEAN Protocol on Enhanced Dispute Settlement Mechanism (2004).

[55] Art. 15(6), ASEAN Protocol on Enhanced Dispute Settlement Mechanism (2004).

[56] Art. 15(2), ASEAN Protocol on Enhanced Dispute Settlement Mechanism (2004).

[57] Art. 19, ASEAN Charter.

[58] Consensus applies where e.g. the SEOM decides by consensus not to adopt a panel report: Art. 9, ASEAN Protocol on Enhanced Dispute Settlement Mechanism (2004).

Chapter 8

Conclusions

Assessing the internal effects of ASEAN external relations

ASEAN's external agreements take many different shapes. They come under different headings and they involve both ASEAN as a distinct entity and its ten Member States as parties on one side of the external agreement. The practice continues to show uncertainties, and it remains in flux.

We have structured our exposition of the internal effects of external agreements along the lines of three different types of such agreements: those with ASEAN as an international organisation as the party to the agreement (Chapter 6) and those that have ASEAN Member States as parties, as plurilateral agreements (Chapter 5) or, in a different reading, as joint agreements (Chapter 6). We have explored the internal effects broadly, to include direct and indirect legal effects as well as effects on the workings of the relationship between ASEAN and its members and between the members themselves. External agreements, we submit, have a bearing on all these relationships.

The overall assessment of the internal effects of ASEAN external agreements, first of all, needs to connect to the type of agreement. If it has the international organisation ASEAN alone as a party, our inquiry shows rather clearly that such agreements do not bind Member States.[1] If members are not themselves parties to the agreement, they could only become bound by ASEAN agreements due to a provision to that effect in the Charter or in a similar document. While such a provision is lacking and cannot be seen on an even distant horizon, this does not conclude the question of internal effects within the ASEAN legal regime. Notably, we drew attention to members' concurrent and subsidiary responsibility and indirect liability for actions of ASEAN as an IO. Should ASEAN incur financial obligations, for instance, by having to pay damages for a wrongful act, there is a compelling argument that members are indirectly liable.[2]

We set out the internal effects of those external agreements, which clearly have the members themselves as a party, on the basis that this is a matter of both international and domestic law. The backdrop of the assessment here is the insight that general international law, in contrast to European law, does not demand to be given direct effect.[3] That is not to question that domestic law cannot justify any acts that are internationally wrongful. Furthermore, some international treaties, such as international trade law, see non-conforming domestic measures as an actionable breach in itself.[4] This view from international law goes hand in hand with the fact that domestic orders can and do give direct effect to international law.[5] Domestic orders that opt to do so (oftentimes called 'monist') would typically do so for *some* international law, especially human rights law, and for other treaties under

---

[1] Section 3.5.   [2] Section 3.6.   [3] Section 4.2.   [4] Section 4.3.
[5] Section 4.5.

further conditions such as, that they create individual rights and that they are sufficiently precise. Treaties would need to be self-executing. International institutions such as international courts can of course themselves pronounce on these conditions, thus trying to influence the effect of treaties within domestic constitutional orders. Other domestic legal orders (oftentimes called 'dualist') demand that international law, before it can be applied directly, be transformed or incorporated. Such incorporation is typically not always done by legislation, but also delegated to administrative-executive procedures.

International agreements oftentimes show significant internal effects in the sphere of interpretation. Such *indirect* effects stem from rules and practices demanding that internal measures be interpreted in conformity with international legal obligations wherever possible. Whereas ASEAN countries differ in their domestic legal orders, including more elements of either monist or dualist systems, they by and large recognise the need for harmonious and consistent interpretation.[6] Since here, too, practices are in some flux, we discussed the policy reasons for and against a strong principle of consistent interpretation.

Especially for economic actors outside ASEAN – be they investors, producers or service-providers – it will be interesting to see how ASEAN members might differ in their internal treatment of external agreements. They could possibly have more opportunity to challenge unfavourable practices in one jurisdiction than another. Such differences

---

[6] Section 4.6.

might then be difficult to square with ASEAN's ambition towards increased economic integration.

Greater harmony among the practices of ASEAN members could arguably result from the implications of joint ASEAN agreements. Like plurilateral agreements, they have ASEAN members as the parties on one side. But ASEAN here makes a difference. Especially if compliance with external agreements was deemed an obligation of membership, members' institutions might end up giving greater internal effect (indirectly, usually) to external agreements. What is more, the ASEAN Secretariat is likely to receive a boost from external agreements that task it with informational, implementing, facilitating and monitoring functions. Arguably, non-compliance with joint external agreements, if it also amounts to a breach of membership, could trigger internal non-compliance and even dispute settlement mechanisms that would run in parallel to the mechanisms that the external agreement itself possibly sets up. It is remarkable, finally, that the 2012 rules of procedure for requesting the ASEAN Secretariat to interpret the ASEAN Charter give the Secretariat considerable interpretative autonomy and authority. In principle, this places the Secretariat into a position to further shape members' obligations and to bear on the effects that external agreements have within the ASEAN legal regime.

Executive summary

The present contribution deals with the effect of ASEAN external relations within the ASEAN legal regime and the legal orders of ASEAN Member States. On the face of it, such effects could be expected to be the same as those of international law generally. But we find that *ASEAN external agreements are likely to have stronger internal effects within Member States than other international law instruments. Furthermore, they contribute to ASEAN integration and may boost the role of the ASEAN Secretariat.*

Our argument is based on an analysis of the obligations of membership in ASEAN and on the principle of ASEAN centrality. Whether compliance with external agreements forms part of the obligations of membership is certainly open to question. We submit that it does, at least with regard to those external agreements that can be read as 'joint ASEAN agreements'. Furthermore, we draw attention to the role that the ASEAN Secretariat itself may play in developing an answer in that direction. The principle of ASEAN centrality is emphasized in a number of key instruments, including the ASEAN Charter. It is likely to contribute to the stronger impact that ASEAN legal instruments may have on the practice of members' institutions when compared to instruments of international law generally.

In order to frame the discussion on internal effects, the contribution distinguishes three types of ASEAN external agreements: (i) external *agreements of ASEAN as an IO*, (ii) *plurilateral agreements* between state parties that resemble any other international treaty, and (iii) *joint ASEAN agreements* between state parties, which however credits the fact that state parties on one side of the agreement together form ASEAN.

i. For the time being, external agreements of the first type – concluded by ASEAN as an IO alone – *do not bind Member States*. Such bindingness could only arise from a provision to that effect in the Charter. Agreements of this type may however strengthen the monitoring, facilitating and compliance functions of the Secretariat with respect to the treaty obligations of Member States. Within the context of this first type of agreements, we also discuss the responsibility of ASEAN and the concurrent and subsidiary responsibility of its members. In particular, we submit that members may be indirectly liable for wrongful acts of ASEAN as an IO.

ii. Plurilateral agreements would be treated like any other international treaty. They do not *claim* to be *directly effective* but might be *given* direct effect depending on the choices made in domestic law, be it at the constitutional, statutory or executive policy level. There is no general obligation to give them direct effect. How domestic law treats them is typically discussed in terms of monism and dualism. The former, monism, in principle allows for direct effect in the sense that agreement provisions have juridical status within the domestic legal order. The latter, dualism, requires that international law be transformed into domestic law before it can be applied, usually by an act of legislative or administrative incorporation. These are approximate models. There is no country within ASEAN or beyond that grants direct effect to all of international law. Relevant factors commonly include whether the international agreement is sufficiently precise, whether it was intended to have direct effect, and whether it creates rights for individuals. This contribution argues that the distinction between monism and dualism has lost most of its explanatory purchase. It belittles the fact that almost all domestic legal orders demand that, wherever fairly possible, domestic instruments should be interpreted in conformity with international law. We call this an *indirect effect*. The distinction between monism and dualism is further overshadowed by the fact that the kind of agreement usually matters more than the domestic constitutional ordering: is the agreement focused on reciprocal rights between states, the relationship between states and individuals, or on the relationships between private parties?

iii. The internal effect of joint ASEAN agreements is threefold. First, where their *direct effect* is concerned, they do not differ from plurilateral agreements and general international law. Second, due to membership obligations and the principle of ASEAN centrality, their *indirect effect* is likely to be stronger. Third, joint ASEAN agreements impact the relationship between ASEAN as a separate entity and its Member States. In particular, they trigger the Secretariat's functions of monitoring and facilitating compliance. Those functions, we note, are all the more important because ASEAN Member States may differ in the way they give effect to their commitments arising out of external agreements. The Secretariat can act with some degree of autonomy to work towards the harmonisation between different approaches among ASEAN Member States.

It matters that part of the state parties to international agreements collectively form ASEAN. Where the monitoring and facilitating role of the Secretariat in external relations is concerned, it merits emphasis that the role of the Secretary-General is further strengthened through the engagement of that office in external relations. While it might be expected that ASEAN internal agreements – especially the Charter – support the view that the Secretariat has a role to play in external relations, the opposite is oftentimes the case: external agreements further support the role and functions of the Secretariat with respect to external relations where these agreements designate it as a depository of ratifications, as a focal point for information exchange, or explicitly as a monitoring body.

This contribution suggests reading most of ASEAN's external agreements as joint ASEAN agreements rather than plurilateral agreements. Such a reading conforms better to the aspirations of ASEAN and to the principle of ASEAN centrality. The notion of joint ASEAN agreements also makes sense of a host of phenomena that cannot easily be brushed aside as mere symbolism.

Abbott, K. W. and D. Snidal, 'Hard and Soft Law in International Governance' (2000) 54 *International Organization* 421–456.

Ahlborn, C., 'The Rules of International Organizations and the Law of International Responsibility' (2011) 8 *International Organizations Law Review* 397, 469.

Alexandrov, S. A., 'Enforcement of ICSID Awards: Articles 53 and 54 of the ICSID Convention', in C. Binder et al. (eds.), *International Investment Law for the 21st Century: Essays in Honour of Christoph Schreuer* (Oxford: Oxford University Press, 2009).

Alì, A., 'Some Reflections on the Principle of Consistent Interpretation through the Case Law of the European Court of Justice', in N. Boschiero et al. (eds.), *International Courts and the Development of International Law: Essays in Honour of Tullio Treves* (Berlin: Springer, 2013) 881–895.

Alias, A. and S. Lutchman, ASEAN ITL Project, Country Report on Malaysia.

van Alstine, M. P., 'The Role of Domestic Courts in Treaty Enforcement: Summary and Conclusions', in D. Sloss (ed.), *The Role of Domestic Courts in Treaty Enforcement: A Comparative Study* (Cambridge: Cambridge University Press, 2009) 555–613.

Alter, K. J., L. R. Helfer and O. Saldías, 'Transplanting the European Court of Justice: The Experience of the Andean Tribunal of Justice' (2012) 60 *American Journal of Comparative Law* 629–664.

Alvarez, J. E., 'Institutionalised Legislation and the Asia-Pacific Region' (2007) 5 *New Zealand Journal of Public and International Law* 9–28.

Amerasinghe, C. F., 'Liability to Third Parties of Member States of International Organizations: Practice, Principle and Judicial Precedent' (1991) 85 *American Journal of International Law* 259–280.

Amrhein-Hofmann, C., *Monismus und Dualismus in den Völkerrechtslehren* (Berlin: Duncker & Humblot, 2003).

Archer, C., *International Organizations*, 3rd edn. (London: Routledge, 2001).

Aust, A., 'United Kingdom', in D. Sloss (ed.), *The Role of Domestic Courts in Treaty Enforcement: A Comparative Study* (Cambridge: Cambridge University Press, 2009) 476–503.

   Modern Treaty Law and Practice (Cambridge: Cambridge University Press, 2007).

Bauer, S., 'Does Bureaucracy Really Matter? The Authority of Intergovernmental Treaty Secretariats in Global Environmental Politics' (2006) 6 *Global Environmental Politics* 24–49.

Benvenisti, E., 'Reclaiming Democracy: The Strategic Uses of Foreign and International Law by National Courts' (2008) 102 *American Journal of International Law* 241–274.

Betlem G. and A. Nollkaemper, 'Giving Effect to Public International Law and European Community Law before Domestic Courts: A Comparative Analysis of the Practice of Consistent Interpretation' (2003) 14 *European Journal of International Law* 569–589.

Binder, C., 'The Prohibition of Amnesties by the Inter-American Court of Human Rights', in A. von Bogdandy and I. Venzke (eds.), *International Judicial Lawmaking: On Public Authority and Democratic Legitimation in Global Governance* (Berlin: Springer, 2012).

von Bogdandy, A., 'Pluralism, Direct Effect, and the Ultimate Say: On the Relationship between International and Domestic Constitutional Law' (2008) 6 *International Journal of Constitutional Law* 397–413.

'Legal Effects of World Trade Organization Decisions within European Union Law: A Contribution to the Theory of the Legal Acts of International Organizations and the Action for Damages under Article 288(2) EC' (2005) 39 *Journal of World Trade* 45–66.

von Bogdandy, A. and J. Bast, 'The Federal Order of Competences', in A. von Bogdandy and J. Bast (eds.), *Principles of EU Constitutional Law* (Oxford and Munich: Hart and Beck, 2009) 275–308.

von Bogdandy, A. and M. Smrkolj, 'European Community and Union Law and International Law', in R. Wolfrum (ed.), *Max Planck Encyclopedia of Public International Law* (Oxford: Oxford University Press, 2012).

von Bogdandy, A. and I. Venzke, 'In Whose Name? An Investigation of International Courts' Public Authority and Its Democratic Justification' (2012) 23 *European Journal of International Law* 7–41.

Bonafé, B. I., 'Direct Effect of International Agreements in the EU Legal Order: Does It Depend on the Existence of an International Dispute Settlement Mechanism?', in E. Cannizzaro, P. Palchetti and R. A. Wessel (eds.), *International Law as Law of the European Union* (The Hague: Martinus Nijhoff, 2012) 229–248.

Boon, K. E., 'New Directions in Responsibility: Assessing the International Law Commission's Draft Articles on the Responsibility of International Organizations' (2011) 37 *Yale Journal of International Law* 1–10.

Bradley, C. A., 'Self-Execution and Treaty Duality' (2008) Supreme Court Review 131–182.

'The Charming Betsy Canon and Separation of Powers: Rethinking the Interpretive Role of International Law' (1997) 86 *Georgetown Law Journal* 479–537.

Brölmann, C., *The Institutional Veil in Public International Law: International Law and the Law of Treaties* (Portland, OR: Hart, 2007) 214.

'The 1986 Vienna Convention on the Law of Treaties: The History of Draft Article 36bis', in J. Klabbers and R. Lefeber (eds.), *Essays on the Law of Treaties: A Collection of Essays in Honour of Bert Vierdag* (The Hague: Martinus Nijhoff, 1998).

Buergenthal, T., 'Self-Executing and Non-Self-Executing Treaties in National and International Law' (1992) 235 *Recueil des Cours* 303.

Cassese, A., *International Law* (Oxford: Oxford University Press, 2005) 218.

Chalmers, D. and L. Barroso, 'What Van Gend en Loos Stands For' (2014) 12 *International Journal of Constitutional Law* 105–134.

Chesterman, S., 'Does ASEAN Exist? The Association of Southeast Asian Nations as an International Legal Person' (2008) 12 *Singapore Year Book of International Law* 199–211.

Choi, S., 'Judicial Enforcement of Arbitration Awards under the ICSID and New York Conventions' (1995–1996) 28 *NYU Journal of International Law & Politics* 175–216.

Chun Hung, L., 'ASEAN Charter: Deeper Regional Integration under International Law' (2010) 9 *Chinese Journal of International Law* 821–837.

Churchill, R. and G. Ulfstein, 'Autonomous Institutional Arrangements in Multilateral Environmental Arrangements: A Little-Noticed Phenomenon in International Law' (2000) 94 *American Journal of International Law* 623–659.

Craig, P., 'The Legal Effect of Directives: Policy, Rules and Exceptions' (2009) *European Law Review* 349–377.

Craig, P. and G. de Búrca, *EU Law*, 4th edn. (Oxford: Oxford University Press, 2007).

Cremona, M., P. Vennesson and R. Lee 'The External Agreements of ASEAN – Inventory and Typology', ASEAN ITL Project, Draft (2013).

d'Aspremont, J., 'Abuse of the Legal Personality of International Organizations and the Responsibility of Member States' (2007) 4 *International Organization Law Review* 91–119.

Davidson, P. J., 'The Role of International Law in the Governance of International Economic Relations in ASEAN' (2008) 12 *Singapore Year Book of International Law* 213–224.

Desierto, D. A., 'ASEAN's Constitutionalization of International Law: Challenges to Evolution under the New ASEAN Charter' (2010) 49 *Columbia Journal of Transnational Law* 268–320.

Desierto, D., ASEAN ITL Project, Country Report on the Philippines.

Dugard, J., South Africa, in D. Sloss (ed.), *The Role of Domestic Courts in Treaty Enforcement: A Comparative Study* (Cambridge: Cambridge University Press, 2009) 448–475.

Dupuy, P.-M., 'International Law and Domestic (Municipal) Law', in R. Wolfrum (ed.), *Max Planck Encyclopedia of Public International Law* (Oxford: Oxford University Press, 2012).

Dupuy, P.-M. and C. Hoss, 'LaGrand Case (Germany v United States of America)', in R. Wolfrum (ed.), *Max Planck Encyclopedia of Public International Law* (Oxford: Oxford University Press, 2009).

Duxbury, A., 'Moving Towards or Turning Away from Institutions?' (2007) 11 *Singapore Year Book of International Law* 177–193.

Eckes, C., 'International Law as Law of the EU. The Role of the European Court of Justice', in E. Cannizzaro, P. Palchetti and R. A. Wessel (eds.), *International law as law of the European Union* (The Hague: Martinus Nijhoff, 2012) 353–377.

Economides, C. P., 'Content of the Obligation: Obligations of Means and Obligations of Result', in J. Crawford, A. Pellet, and S. Olleson (eds.), *The Law of International Responsibility* (Oxford: Oxford University Press, 2010) 371–381.

Eeckhout, P., *EU External Relations Law* (Oxford: Oxford University Press, 2011).

Ehlermann, C.-D., 'Mixed Agreements – A List of Problems', in Keeffe and Schermers (eds.), *Mixed Agreements* (Leiden: Kluwer, 1983).

Finegan, T., 'Neither Dualism nor Monism: Holism and the Relationship between Municipal and International Human Rights Law' (2011) 2 *Transnational Legal Theory* 477–503.

Finnemore, M. and S. Toope, 'Alternatives to "Legalization": Richer Views of Law and Politics' (2001) 55 *International Organization* 743–758.

Fleuren, J., 'The Application of Public International Law by Dutch Courts' (2010) 57 *Netherlands International Law Review* 245–266.

Foster, C. and V. Jivan, *Gender Equality Laws: Global Good Practice and a Review of Five Southeast Asian Countries* (Bangkok: UNIFEM, 2009).

Friedmann, W. G., *The Changing Structure of International Law* (New York, Columbia University Press, 1964).

Gaja, G., 'Dualism: A Review', in J. Nijman and A. Nollkaemper (eds.), *New Perspectives on the Divide between National and International Law* (Oxford: Oxford University Press, 2007) 52–62.

Gärditz, F., 'Die Legitimation der Justiz zur Völkerrechtsfortbildung' (2008) 47 *Der Staat* 381–409.

Gazzini, T., 'The Relationship between International Legal Personality and the Autonomy of International Organisations', in E. Collins and N. White (eds.), *International Organizations and the Idea of Autonomy: Institutional Independence in the International Legal Order* (Abingdon, Oxon: Routledge, 2011) 97–141.

Ghafur Hamdi, A. and K. Maung Sein, 'Judicial Application of International Law in Malaysia' (2005) 1 *Asia Pacific Yearbook of International Law* 196–214.

Goldmann, M., 'We Need to Cut Off the Head of the King: Past, Present, and Future Approaches to International Soft Law' (2012) 25 *Leiden Journal of International Law* 335–368.

Goldstein, J., M. Kahler, R. D. Keohane, and A. Slaughter, 'Introduction: Legalization and World Politics' (2000) 54 *International Organization* 385–399.

Groves, M., 'Is Teoh's Case Still Good Law' (2007) 14 *Australian Journal of Administrative Law* 126.

Haftel, Y. Z. and A. Thompson, 'The Independence of International Organizations: Concept and Applications' (2006) 50 *Journal of Conflict Resolution* 253–275.

Hamdi, A. G. and K. M. Sein, 'Judicial Application of International Law in Malaysia' (2005) 1 *Asia Pacific Yearbook of International Law* 196–214.

Hartwig, M., 'International Organizations or Institutions, Responsibility and Liability', in R. Wolfrum (ed.), *Max Planck Encyclopedia of Public International Law* (Oxford: Oxford University Press, 2011).

'The International Tin Council (ITC)', in R. Wolfrum (ed.), *Max Planck Encyclopedia of Public International Law* (Oxford: Oxford University Press, 2011).

Die Haftung der Mitgliedstaaten für Internationale Organisationen (Heidelberg: Springer, 1993).

Henkin, L., 'International Law as Law in the United States' (1984) 82 *Michigan Law Review* 1555–1569.

Henry, L., 'When Is a Treaty Self–Executing' (1928) 27 *Michigan Law Review* 776–785.

Herdegen, M., 'The Insolvency of International Organizations and the Legal Position of Creditors: Some Observations in the Light of the International Tin Council Crisis' (1988) 35 *Netherlands International Law Review* 135–144.

Hesselink, M. W., 'A Toolbox for European Judges' (2011) 17 *European Law Journal* 441–469.

Hirsch, M., *The Responsibility of International Organizations Toward Third Parties: Some Basic Principles* (Dordrecht: Martinus Nijhoff, 1995).

Institut de Droit International, 'The Legal Consequences for Member States of the Non-fulfillment by International Organizations of their Obligations toward Third Parties', (1995).

Jackson, J. H., 'Status of Treaties in Domestic Legal Systems: A Policy Analysis' (1992) 86 *American Journal of International Law* 310–340.

Jackson J. H. and A. O. Skyes, *Implementing the Uruguay Round* (Oxford: Clarendon Press, 1997) 461.

Jetschke, A., 'ASEAN', in M. Beeson and R. Stubbs (eds.), *Routledge Handbook of Asian Regionalism*, (Abingdon, Oxon: Routledge, 2012) 327–337.

Kahler, M., 'Legalization as Strategy: The Asia-Pacific Case' (2000) 54 *International Organization* 549–571.

Keller, H., *Rezeption des Völkerrechts* (Berlin: Springer, 2003) 42.

Klabbers, J., *An Introduction to International Institutional Law*, 2nd edn. (Cambridge: Cambridge University Press, 2009).

'Compliance Procedures', in D. Bodansky, J. Brunnée and E. Hey (eds.), *The Oxford Handbook of International Environmental Law* (Oxford: Oxford University Press, 2007).

'Two Concepts of International Organization' (2005) 2 *International Organization Law Review* 277–293.

An Introduction to International Institutional Law (Cambridge: Cambridge University Press, 2002).

Koh, T., W. Woon, and C. Sze-Wei, 'Charter Makes ASEAN Stronger, More United and Effective' *Straits Times (Singapore)*, 8 August 2007.

Koskenniemi, M., 'Breach of Treaty or Non-Compliance? Reflections on the Enforcement of the Montreal Protocol' (1992) 3 *Yearbook of International Environmental Law* 123–162.

Krasner, S. D., 'Structural Causes and Regime Consequences: Regimes as Intervening Variables' (1982) 36 *International Organization* 185–205.

Kratochwil, F., *The Status of Law in World Society: Meditations on the Role and Rule of Law* (Cambridge: Cambridge University Press, 2014) 32–33.

Kuijper, P. J. "'It Shall Contribute to . . . the Strict Observance and Development of International Law. . ." The Role of the Court of Justice', in A. Rosas, E. Levits and Y. Bot (eds.), *The Court of Justice and the Construction of Europe* (The Hague: T. M. C. Asser Press, 2013) 589–612.

'Of "Mixity" and "Double-hatting"' Inaugural Lecture (Vossiuspers UvA, 2008).

Lenaerts, K., 'Direct Applicability and Direct Effect of International Law in the EU Legal Order', in I. Govaere et al. (eds.), *The European Union in the World. Essays in Honour of Marc Maresceau* (Leiden: Brill, 2014) 45–64.

Leviter, L., 'The ASEAN Charter: ASEAN's Failure or Member Failure?' (2010) 43 *Journal of International Law and Politics* 159–210.

Linton, S., 'ASEAN States, Their Reservations to Human Rights Treaties and the Proposed ASEAN Commission on Women and Children' (2008) 30 *Human Rights Quarterly* 436–493.

Malaya, J. E. E. and M. A. Mendoza-Oblena, 'Philippine Treaty Law and Practice' (2010) 35 *Integrated Bar of the Philippines Journal* 1–17.

Martines, F., 'Direct Effect of International Agreements of the European Union' (2014) 25 *European Journal of International Law* 129–147.

Mendes, M., *The Legal Effects of EU Agreements* (Oxford: Oxford University Press, 2013).

Messineo, F., 'Multiple Attribution of Conduct', in A. Nollkaemper and I. Plakokefalos (eds.), *Principles of Shared Responsibility* (Cambridge: Cambridge University Press, 2014).

Murphy, S. D., 'Does International Law Obligate States to Open Their National Courts to Persons for the Invocation of Treaty Norms That Protect or Benefit Persons?' in D. Sloss (ed.), *The Role of Domestic Courts in Treaty Enforcement: A Comparative Study* (Cambridge: Cambridge University Press, 2009) 61–119.

Murray, O., 'Piercing the Corporate Veil: The Responsibility of Member states of an International Organization' (2011) 8 *International Organizations Law Review* 291–347.

Naldi, G. J., 'The ASEAN Protocol on Dispute Settlement Mechanisms: An Appraisal' (2014) 5 *Journal of International Dispute Settlement* 105–138.

Nguyen, L.-A. T. and J. Freeman, ASEAN ITL, Country Report on Vietnam.

Nollkaemper, A., 'The Duality of Direct Effect of International Law' (2014) 25 *European Journal of International Law* 105–125.

National Courts and the International Rule of Law (Oxford: Oxford University Press, 2011).

'The Netherlands', in D. Sloss (ed.), *The Role of Domestic Courts in Treaty Enforcement: A Comparative Study* (Cambridge: Cambridge University Press, 2009) 326–369.

Nollkaemper, A. and J. E. Nijman, 'Beyond the Divide', in A. Nollkaemper and J. E. Nijman (eds.), *New Perspectives on the Divide between National and International Law* (Oxford: Oxford University Press, 2007) 341–360.

Paasivirta, E. and P. J. Kuijper, 'Does One Size Fit All?: The European Community and the Responsibility of International Organizations' (2005) 36 *Netherlands Yearbook of International Law* 169–226.

Paust, J. J., 'Self-Executing Treaties' (1988) 82 *American Journal of International Law* 760–783.

Pauwelyn, J., R. Wessel and J. Wouters (eds.), *Informal International Lawmaking* (Oxford: Oxford University Press, 2012).

Pernice, I., 'Die Haftung internationaler Organisationen und ihrer Mitglieder, dargestellt am 'Fall' des internationalen Zinnrates' (1988) 26 *Archiv des Völkerrechts* 406–433.

Pescatore, P., 'The Doctrine of "Direct Effect": An Infant Disease of Community Law' (1983) 8 *European Law Review* 155.

Peters, A., *Jenseits der Menschenrechte: Die Rechtsstellung des Individuums im Völkerrecht* (Tübingen: Mohr Siebeck, 2014).

Petersmann, E.-U., 'The Judicial Task of Administering Justice in Trade and Investment Law and Adjudication' (2012) 4 *Journal of International Dispute Settlement* 5–28.

Pinseethong, K., ASEAN ITL Project, Country Report on Thailand.

Prechal, S., 'Direct Effect, Indirect Effect, Supremacy and the Evolving Constitution of the European Union', in C. Barnard (ed.), *The Fundamentals of EU Law Revisited: Assessing the Impact of the Constitutional Debate* (Oxford: Oxford University Press, 2007) 35–69.

Directives in EC Law, 2nd edn. (Oxford: Oxford University Press, 2005).

Reinalda, B., 'ASEAN as an Informal Organization: Does It Exist and Does It Have Agency? The Emergence of the ASEAN Secretariat', in J. E. Oestreich (ed.), *International Organizations as Self-Directed Actors* (Abingdon, Oxon: Routledge, 2012).

Reinisch, A., *International Organizations Before National Courts* (Cambridge: Cambridge University Press, 2000).

Roberts, S., 'Minister of State for Immigration and Ethnic Affairs v. Ah Hin Teoh: The High Court Decision and the Government's Reaction To It' (1995) 2 *Australian Journal of Human Rights* 135.

Rothwell, D. R., 'Australia', in D. Sloss (ed.), *The Role of Domestic Courts in Treaty Enforcement: A Comparative Study* (Cambridge: Cambridge University Press, 2009) 120–165.

Ruiz Fabri, H., 'Is There a Case – Legally and Politically – for Direct Effect of WTO Obligations?' (2014) 25 *European Journal of International Law* 151–173.

Ryngaert, C. and H. Buchanan, 'Member State Responsibility for the Acts of International Organizations' (2011) 7 *Utrecht Law Review* 131–146.

Sadurska, R. and C. M. Chinkin, 'The Collapse of the International Tin Council: A Case of State Responsibility?' (1990) 30 *Virginia Journal of International Law* 845–890.

Schermers, H. G. and N. M. Blokker, *International Institutional Law*, 5th edn. (Leiden: Martinus Nijhoff, 2011).

 International Institutional Law, 4th edn. (Leiden: Martinus Nijhoff, 2003).

Schruer, C., 'The Waning of the Sovereign State: Towards a New Paradigm for International Law?' (1993) 4 *European Journal of International Law* 447–471.

Seah, D., 'The ASEAN Charter' (Current Developments) (2009) 58 *International and Comparative Law Quarterly* 212–219.

Seibert-Fohr, A., 'Domestic Implementation of the International Covenant on Civil and Political Rights Pursuant to Its Article 2 para 2' (2001) 5 *Max Planck Yearbook of United Nations Law* 399–472.

Severino, R. C., *Southeast Asia in Search of an ASEAN Community: Insights from the Former ASEAN Secretary-General* (Singapore: ISEAS Publishing, 2006).

Shelton, D., 'Introduction' in D. Shelton (ed.), *International Law and Domestic Legal Systems: Incorporation, Transformation, and Persuasion* (Oxford: Oxford University Press, 2011) 1–22.

Sloss, D., 'Domestic Application of Treaties', in D. Hollis (ed.), *The Oxford Guide to Treaties* (Oxford: Oxford University Press, 2012) 379–388.

Stone Sweet, A. and H. Keller, *A Europe of Rights: The Impact of the ECHR on National Legal Systems* (Oxford: Oxford University Press, 2008).

Stumer, A., 'Liability of Member States for Acts of International Organizations: Reconsidering the Policy Objections' (2007) 48 *Harvard International Law Journal* 553–580.

Tan, E., ASEAN ITL Project, Country Report on Singapore.

Tancredi, A., 'On the Absence of Direct Effect of the WTO Dispute Settlement Body's Decisions in the EU Legal Order', in E. Cannizzaro, P. Palchetti and R. A. Wessel (eds.), *International Law as Law of the European Union* (The Hague: Martinus Nijhoff, 2012) 249–268.

Tiwari, S., (ed.), *Life after the Charter* (Singapore: Institute of SEA Studies, 2009).

Triepel, H., *Völkerrecht und Landesrecht* (Leipzig: Hirschfeldt, 1899).

Vauchez, A., 'The Transnational Politics of Judicialization. Van Gend en Loos and the Making of European Union Polity' (2010) 16 *European Law Journal* 1.

Vazquez, C. M., 'Treaties as Law of the Land: The Supremacy Clause and the Judicial Enforcement of Treaties' (2008) 122 *Harvard Law Review* 599–695.

'The Four Doctrines of Self-Executing Treaties' (1995) 89 *American Journal of International Law* 695–723.

Venzke, I., 'International Bureaucracies in a Political Science Perspective – Agency, Authority and International Institutional Law' (2008) 9 *German Law Journal* 1401–1428.

Weiler, J. H. H., 'The External Legal Relations of Non-Unitary Actors: Mixity and the Federal Principle', in J. H. H. Weiler, *The Constitution of Europe* (Cambridge: Cambridge University Press, 1999) 130–187.

'The Transformation of Europe' (1991) 100 *Yale Law Journal* 2403–2483.

de Witte, B., 'Direct Effect, Primacy and the Nature of the Legal Order', in G. de Búrca and P. Craig (eds.), *The Evolution of European Union Law* (Oxford: Oxford University Press, 2011) 323.

White, N. D., *The Law of International Organizations*, 2nd edn. (Manchester: Manchester University Press, 2005).

Wu, C.-H., 'The ASEAN Economic Community under the ASEAN Charter: Its External Economic Relations and Dispute Settlement Mechanism' (2010) 1 *European Yearbook of International Economic Law* 331–357.

223

Lightning Source UK Ltd.
Milton Keynes UK
UKHW020730210422
401835UK00006B/79